D1273107

COLLECTING MODEL SOLDIERS

BOOKS BY THE SAME AUTHOR

Model Soldiers: A Collector's Guide

Model Soldiers for the Connoisseur

COLLECTING MODEL SOLDIERS

JOHN G. GARRATT

ARCO PUBLISHING COMPANY, INC
NEW YORK

Published by Arco Publishing Company, Inc.
219 Park Avenue South, New York, N.Y. 10003

Library of Congress Catalog Card Number 74-24665

ISBN 0-668-03749-0

Printed in Great Britain

FOR CORNELIUS FRAZER

CONTENTS

LIST OF ILLUSTRATIONS

All models, except where otherwise stated, are in the author's collection and were photographed by Downing Street Studios, Farnham.

INTRODUCTION

The once-gentle hobby of collecting model soldiers has now become a universally popular pastime, and each year sees an increase in the number of collectors in most parts of the world. Many of these are young, have acquired little knowledge of the background of the hobby, or are unconversant with the models of the makers who have made it possible. Indeed, only recently a review of a book on the subject demonstrated that the reviewer was entirely ignorant of the literature that has been published during the last twenty years. That is one reason why this book has been written – to give a balanced assessment of makers past and present.

Another factor worth mentioning is the comparatively recent advent of two completely new schools of model soldier enthusiasts: the converters, and the private makers, or 'freelancers'. These, whilst dependent on the products of the commercial makers, do not of necessity collect specimens, other than to dismember them, but at the same time the skill that they display both in their reassembly and in their painting and presentation forms a large group in the overall picture. However, for reasons of space it is possible to mention only one or two in a book of this nature; indeed, it does not seem possible that any book could be written which would not be invidious in its choice. If these enthusiasts pursue their alterations and improvements for their own pleasure, this should be sufficient reward.

We have been so accustomed to a certain manner of acquiring our models that it might be instructive to go back to the early days of the 1950s, when industry was reshaping itself in all countries after the disastrous interlude of World War II. In this way a truer picture of the present scene will emerge.

In those days there were far more shops selling toys as such than there are today. First, of course, were the large stores devoted entirely to toys of all kinds, or which had special departments devoted to nothing else. Each town had its special type of shop, either selling toys exclusively, or having a large proportion of them. Woolworths were far more enterprising, both in the United States and in England, offering as they did a range of products nowhere else to be found. There were also the queer, dingy places where one could buy picture postcards, tobacco and souvenirs. These were usually family businesses, handed down from generation to generation (or still under the care of the ancient owner) and offered a personal service not often found in these more competitive and sophisticated times.

In all these places one could find model soldiers, or 'toy soldiers' as they were generally known, the quality and variety depending on the prosperity or scope of the respective shop. The lordly one had Britains galore, floor to ceiling stacked with the narrow, oblong boxes. Britains still had the monopoly, but Timpo and Johillco were also very popular makers. Charbens and Cherilea, although far behind in quality, had their devotees, since they manufactured ranges not made by the larger firms. Elastolin models from Germany were in evidence; Heydes and Mignots in their respective countries Germany and France, and in England and the United States. It was in the odd shops that one found the single model, destined to last for a short time before disappearing into oblivion. Some, indeed, were almost museum pieces, and few bore a trade-mark. Here could be found such varieties as those peculiarly clumsy Treforest Mouldings; or the only four styles made by MSR of Brighton; or those figures of a curious material subsequently identified as being made by Malleable Mouldings; or a batch of the ill-fated Authenticast–Comet productions made in Eire; or, on the Left Bank in Paris, a collection of the now rare Palx.

There seemed no logical system of distribution, so that in whichever town one happened to be one might find something new: a Lone Star in Sheffield, a Reynolds in Gloucester, a Carman in a small turning off Covent Garden, a Lincoln Log in Pittsburgh, a McLoughlin in Philadelphia.

Some of the firms were beginning to break away from the traditional boxed sets, and to issue their products (usually half a dozen in a series) in different postures, and in separate pictorial packages, and even Britains succumbed to this practice with their 'Knights of Agincourt'. Going, too, was the old convention of the rigid adherence to so many soldiers performing the same action. This was due to the advancing technology of mould-making which introduced the possibility of more naturalistic poses.

Plastics were beginning to rear what to some is still an ugly head, and at opposite ends of the scale were that survivial of the Dark Ages, the semi-solid, and that new arrival, the large polystyrene kit, commencing with the American Aurora's 'Black Knight of Nuremberg'.

At the same time there were models of a higher quality, although one had to look further for them. Polk's of New York, Hummels and Hamleys in London and Chambon in Paris stocked Ping, Courtenay, Stadden, Greenwood & Ball, Métayer, Gammage, Carman, and Niblett, and the plaster models of Willetts and the Sentry Box. There was a great gulf between them and the models on sale in other shops.

As to collecting, this was a matter of personal preference. The rich man bought the best pieces (and these would be already painted), or whatever took his fancy, whether a connoisseur, a hollow-cast, or a plastic model. The less rich were happy with the humbler models; the Britains fanatic bought Britains only. There were societies in New York and Pennsylvania and Washington, in London, Paris, Amsterdam and Vienna. Membership of each was about three or four hundred; staid sessions were held monthly; annual competitions were limited to perhaps half a dozen classes, and great excitement was caused by the formation of a regional branch. The only unpainted castings available were those of Britains, made available to members of the British society through the kind offices of the manufacturer. Few messed about with scalpels or soldering irons, and there were hardly any commercial aids to converting. There were no periodicals to review monthly a new batch of models fresh from the maker's moulds; one kept in touch with world events by means of the journal of whichever society one belonged to. Illustrations of uniforms were not easily obtainable, and recourse had to be made to the nearest reference library.

Dioramas were made, on the whole, for special events; exhibitions were few, and attracted what today would seem a ridiculously small audience. The wargame was taking its first tentative steps. However, in those days no one had the temerity to pontificate on how one should paint or alter one's models, and it was all a pleasant diversion from the stress of life.

Today, the only factor in common is the attitude of the press and television – it was and still is somewhat patronising, prepared to admit that there must be something in it, but at the same time not prepared to be serious. But today the cult of the model soldier in all countries is far from being a joke; nobody could be more serious than a collector of these fascinating little figures.

Finally a warning to the reader. The rate at which model soldiers of all sizes and media, in all countries, are being produced means that no author could possibly keep up with the latest productions. The best he can do is to indicate what is available at the time of writing, and hope that the reader will have gained sufficient enthusiasm to pursue investigations for himself.

I

THE BEGINNINGS

The making of figurines of a military nature goes back to antiquity, and its history has already been recorded in detail in several standard works of reference. Only a very brief résumé of the important historical aspects is necessary here.

The commercial ancestors of the present-day models are the 'solids' and the 'flats'. The former evolved naturally from small, round, lead objects, and were for the first time manufactured in bulk by Lucotte of Paris, a firm which was taken over in 1858 by Cuperly, Blondel and Gerbeau, and later still by Mignot (who still retain the trademark C.B.G.). The characteristics were weightiness and completely round design allied to excellent detail and anatomy. The superior class Lucottes were cast solid from a mould with accoutrements, horse furniture and rider cast separately, whereas the lesser quality Mignots were (and are) cast in one piece. The idea of solid, substantial models was seized upon by the Germans, and in George Heyde they found a commercial manufacturer as important as Lucotte. Although anatomically far behind the French, these German models, by reason of their massive output and variety, were immediately popular, and have remained so. Far better in quality were the products of the firm of Haffner, a few of which are museum pieces. All these Germanic products were prolific in England at the end of the nineteenth century, mixed with an atrocious hybrid known as the 'semi-solid', usually of much smaller size.

The earliest of any commercial models were tiny silhouette-like figures, emanating from such towns as Nuremberg and

Furth. The first manufacturer to recognise the potential of these 'flats' was Johannes Hilpert in the 1750s. His influence lasted until well into the mid-nineteenth century, when his natural successor, Ernst Heinrichsen, laid the foundations both in size and scope for the interest in these fascinating little figures which is still such an important part of the model soldier world.

Sandwiched in between the solids and the flats are the paper sheets. Beginning as copper engravings to illustrate books on military matters, they soon developed into separate publications of representations of uniforms to be coloured, cut out, and stuck on to tiny wooden blocks. Some were coloured and heightened with gold by the publishers, mainly of course, for royal patrons. Lithography and, later, colour lithography, led to the issue of thousands of sheets, especially in such French centres as Nancy, Epinal and Strasbourg. The practice of cutting out the figures has now been abandoned (although some modern sheets are pre-pressed for punching out), and the sheets carefully preserved. A separate volume is necessary to examine in detail the rich variety that is contained in these examples of graphic and folk art.

Up to the 1890s the field was held by German flats, hybrids and solids, and French solids, and in no other countries had any attempt been made to build up a native industry. However, in England a certain William Britain, already an established maker of mechanical toys, turned his attention to the making of model soldiers. To try to compete with the Continent by making solids was obviously suicidal, but Britain was convinced that there would be a market for a cheaper production if it were well made.

In 1893, after several years of experiment, his solution was placed on the market. In essence what he had done was to make a model consisting of two pieces of thin lead alloy which, when joined together, enclosed a vacuum, thus eliminating the need for a large quantity of heavy metal and consequently reducing the cost of production. Just as Heinrichsen set a new pattern by his 28mm flats, Britain was the originator of a standing figure of 54mm, thus enabling prospective purchasers to be assured that there would be no anomalous sized figures in their collections. (Britain was to break this rule occasionally, issuing some cheaper models in smaller and some more expensive ones in larger sizes.)

Careful research ensured that these 'hollow-casts' were accurate to a degree; the painting was carried out competently at the factory by teams of home workers, in the manner traditional to British manufacturers of many different types of goods of the period. (An earlier parallel may be cited, that of the hand-colouring of aquatints and lithographs. One set of colourists filled in the sky and the foreground, another the houses and trees, yet another the ships, people etc. In the case of fashion prints, one dealt with hats and bonnets, another with the dresses, another with the ribbons, parasols, and the like.) I visited Britains factory and saw the painting in action. One girl had two hundred or so cavalrymen in front of her and was applying a coat of black paint to each of the horses. Another had a similar number of infantry, and was painting in the 'blushes' on the already pink cheeks, whilst at the next table gold stripes were being applied to otherwise completed models.

These hollow-casts, far more accurate, easier to handle, more attractive, and cheaper than their German and French counterparts, and above all concentrating on types and regiments of the British Army, at first met with resistance from the conservative toyshops. However, this resistance gradually died away, and the now familiar boxes, each containing the same number of infantry or mounted figures, and much more easily purchasable and storable than the German models, began to appear in all the large shops. Within five years popularity was assured, and within ten the Germans had been swept from the board. The gamble had succeeded.

Whilst Britains remained faithful to their British Army plan, they did at the same time occasionally make models of the troops of other countries, minor, local wars providing the excuse. Models were redesigned and improved as the years went by, and experiments made in construction and in the use of materials. Artillery and ambulances were added, together with civilian and farming activities for the non-military minded. It has always remained a regret that with all their activity Britains never showed the enterprise of their continental rivals in the sphere of periods earlier than the nineteenth and twentieth centuries.

The fascination of Britains' models for the collector is not, therefore, their world-wide variety, but the variations that occur within self-imposed limits. As has just been stated, the first models were being constantly remade either because of anatomical peculiarities or to bring them up to date with the changing uniforms of the times. There were experiments also with such things as fixed and movable arms (including one where a shaft extended right through the figure from one side to the other) and with a weapon fitted to the hand by a plug – the 'plughanded Highlander'. Some early swords were of pure tin-plate; bases were either round, oval or oblong.

It is necessary to acquire the various 'issues' or 'states' to complete collections. The avid Britains' enthusiast will need to look for the first version (1899–c1913) of the naval landing party, the second version (c1913–39) with stockier sailors, and the third version (1939–62) where the wheels of the gun and limber are thicker. There are variations among the 'standing firing', 'standing at the ready', 'kneeling to receive a cavalry charge', and 'at the slope' of the buglers and the drummer boys; the trousers of French zouaves at various dates; the anatomy of the chests of modern Greek troops, and even in the position of the feet of the 'lying firing' models.

Horses were 'cross-legged' or 'one-eared'; there was a style known as the 'rocking horse', and another is designated a 'pony horse'; the first version of the Bikanir and the Egyptian Camel Corps had a camel with a wire tail, which was later cast in lead. A line officer first appeared with a small head and a wasp waist: the same waist differs in the first and second version of a nursing sister. Although the 21st Hussars were changed to Lancers in 1897–8, Britains made at least four different versions, incorporating changes in the uniform that took place after the regiment ceased to exist! Variations of the kind mentioned occur right through Britains' career, and the enthusiast cannot do better than acquire L. W. Richard's *Old British Lead Soldiers*, where details are given of practically every model that was made.

Britains' output up to 1967, when they were forced to discontinue the making of hollow-casts, must have been phenomenal. By the very nature of their construction the models were particularly susceptible to breakage, as many a matchstick mend or a re-gluing shows. Even so, there are still thousands of models in well-preserved order in private collections all over the world, carefully handed down from father to son such was the prestige they enjoyed. Every now and then these come on the market, and fetch prices out of all proportion to their intrinsic qualities. Stripped of their nostalgic glamour, they are still toys, but no one would deny them their historic importance as the first models to really grip the British in a vice that has never slackened. It is, of course, possible that the new metal figures issued by Britains in 1973 will achieve the same popularity as their forefathers.

Britains naturally had soon to contend with rivals who quickly mastered the hollow-cast process and began to turn out models in slavish imitation or even in some cases downright forgery – in fact, one or two were successfully prosecuted. On the other hand not all the specimens were piracies, and at times figures not to be found elsewhere emanated from these smaller firms, especially in the civilian ranges. These rivals (Fry, Renvoize, Hanks, Reka, W. T. Courtenay, Taylor & Barratt, Wood, W & C, Turnbull and the like) have, on the whole little to recommend them. The firm of BMC, however, with 60mm models, were superior to most, and must be noted as one of the exceptions. The much better known firm of Johillco also more than held its own with Britains over many years, and whilst specialising in the same type of material, at times produced an acceptable and unusual figure, and went further into the field of Romans, gladiators, crusaders, Arabs and the like.

Johillco and Britains were the only firms to recommence business after World War II, and they were joined by a number of others, most of whom displayed a far greater variety, especially in the positions of their figures. Timpo, for example, concentrated on differences rather than uniformity. Their American GIs were in all types of postures, even off-duty ones, which formed the basis of many a conversion. Slightly larger (56mm) and more solid than Britains' models, they had a sturdy dependability and on the whole were well designed and cast. Apart from modern troops, of which there were many varieties, they made Romans (not up to standard) and medieval models. Perhaps for the first time a good solid horse, capable of carrying armour, was produced. Their 'Ivanhoe' and 'Arthur' sets were issued with detachable riders, an innovation with hollow-cast models. The lances were originally made of metal, but frailty at the hand-grip led to their replacement by inferior plastic ones. The 'Quentin Durward' set was also a notable achievement.

Crescent, though normally designing an indifferent model, occasionally came up with something out of the ordinary, as for instance a Black Prince, detachable, the same horse serving also for a Duke of Marlborough. Most interesting of all was a charging, caparisoned horse by Cherilea; the knight although poor in design, had a removable yet overlarge helm, and lance, battle-axe and sword, were all interchangeable.

The firm of Charbens, again, whilst on the whole quite negligible, still from time to time attracted the attention with a model outside the range of the other makers, as did Reynolds, who produced an admirably stocky set of Danes, and Kews, producing quite a range of varied models. A rarity is a set of four models, not particularly well designed, from an engineering firm MSR, operating from a back-street in Brighton. Lone Star, made a few ranges, and altogether the period is a fascinating one, not so much for the quality of the models, as for the discovery of hitherto unrecognised makers.

Meanwhile, on the Continent, hollow-cast methods were being adopted by both Heyde and Mignot, but mainly for their cheaper lines. The solid model, was still the most popular, as evinced by the productions of Emanuel Steinback (MIM) in Belgium, Andersen (Brigader) in Sweden, Casanellas (La Guerra), Palomeque, and Sanquez in Spain, and Antonini (Figir) and I.S.A. in Italy. All these countries imported Britains', Heydes and Mignots; continental flats, semi-flats and semi-solids were also greatly in evidence.

The United States were content to rely on British and foreign manufactures. They themselves had made a few isolated flats of poor quality in the late nineteenth century, but it was not until the early twentieth century that any real effort was made to produce a native industry, and the influence of Heyde is to be seen in the works of McLoughlin Brothers, the American Soldier Company, Barclay, and the Grey Iron Casting Company, all of whose models were of poor quality. McLoughlin is also known to have issued paper sheets. One of the earliest makers to attempt to improve the standard was Moulded Miniatures (1929) and with their advent, together with Trucraft, the Minifigure Company and Military Miniatures (who closed down about 1950) the first native American school may be said to have emerged, especially as they endeavoured to portray their own native armies in their various wars. They were later joined by an old-established firm, Comet, who later, and by rare good fortune, obtained the services of the renowned Holger Eriksson to design their now famous 'Authenticast' group.

2

THE EMERGENCE OF THE MASTERS

By now there were many serious collectors of model soldiers who were dissatisfied with the models on the market. They were beginning to demand something better, and they themselves attempted to influence producers. Not for them were the mass-produced solids or hollow-casts: their ideal was an artist-designed, solid-cast model, individually made to their own particular taste. This desire had always been inherent in France, and had evinced itself at odd times during the commercial era, but it was not until the 1920s that it really manifested itself. Early in the field was Marcel Baldet, whose hand-made, specially commissioned models are in many French and Canadian collections. With him was Auger and Bittard, both of whom naturally glorified the French Napoleonic armies. Madame Métayer was another collector dissatisfied with the commercial field, and by her efforts in conjunction with Lucien Rousselot she raised the standard of production, whilst still preserving her integrity. Since those early days she has produced many outstanding models, and has been in great demand for diorama work, often in collaboration with Eugène Lelièpvre.

The French idea was, and still is, the use of a basic torso on which to build a figure by means of successive applications of solder or thinnest sheet lead. True, the legs of horses may be cast in separate pieces, and then soldered together, and equipment, heads and the like also made in separate moulds, but the emphasis is on the unique figure which can only be made by the soldering together of a number of components. Reins, plumes for helmets, trumpet cords, buttons, swords and slings, are all made as individual units, and the whole amalgamated together into one graceful model.

One of the earliest and finest exponents of the art in France (happily still working, as indeed, are many of the others) is Roger Berdou. He has over the years created a legend for himself, by his own reticence, and his clients are few but life-long. Each model that he produces is a miracle of accuracy, proportion, anatomy, grace and elegant painting. Each contains perhaps seventy different solderings, taking months to make. Berdou undertakes one model at a time, to which he devotes his whole attention until it is completed. A careful record is then made of every detail, so that no client will ever receive a model that has been repeated in any possible way. Collectors are so aware of the responsibilities of owning Berdou's models that they are rarely exhibited, but they are spoken about in collectors' circles with bated breath.

Mademoiselle des Fontaines has a wider range of interest, as evinced by such divergent models as a series of ancient chariots, Napoleon riding a camel, an armed elephant, a medieval hawking pair, and various individuals of the American War of Independence. She too is kept fully occupied by commissions. Her models have been seen at Polk's Hobby Store, and at the annual exhibitions of the French and British societies, and she and Berdou represent all that is best in connoisseur models. I have never seen a model by Bernard Vanot, who started as a protégé of Lelièpvre, but I am assured that he also is in the highest class. Lelièpvre, himself the author of many fine figures in varied media, has greatly influenced the development of the model soldier in many directions, both by his own models and his encouragement of other, younger artists. His latest venture (1973) is a series of twelve fine models, designed for Jean Montagne, of the battle of Austerlitz, with the figures marketed on a subscription basis.

In Sweden, in his quiet but authoritative way, Holger

Eriksson began casting his models from a single mould, from which he raised the standard to previously unthought of heights. He was an innovator in sizes too, making not only the normal 54mm, but models in 30mm and 40mm also. His models have a distinctly sculpturesque quality not often to be found elsewhere.

It was in England, however, that the greatest demand for a better model was found, and Richard Courtenay was one of the first in the field. He had already gained experience in casting by an association with E. Doran, in a short range of small-size medieval commercial models, and he was now able to indulge his own passion for this particular period. He made himself master of this era, and for those collectors attuned to his ideals there will never be a maker to equal him. He held the field from about 1925 to his death in 1964, and was complemented rather than challenged by Ping, who indeed collaborated with him on a number of designs. More recently other makers, inspired by the attraction of armour and colour, have turned their hands to recreating the period. Even though they may be as accurate in their heraldry as Courtenay, as bright in their painting or more furious in their action, they still seem to miss something that Courtenay had, and his indefinable magic emerges enhanced by comparison. Highly accomplished as these other models undoubtedly are, and well worthy of acceptance, by even the most hypercritical of collectors, there is always a slight heaviness about them, a feeling that their intent is perhaps a ponderous display of erudition and a theatrical atmosphere that emphasises the innate grace of a Courtenay conception. Perhaps there is a reticent in a Courtenay. His models certainly have a dancing fluidity that one cannot find elsewhere.

Courtenay's original sketches and his historical and heraldic notes reveal that the final model was achieved not without much thought and hard endeavour. Peter Greenhill drew my attention to the significance of Courtenay's first efforts when working with Doran. These early models (in which the armour itself incidentally, was left unpainted) have up till now been rather disdainfully dismissed by collectors, and certainly they display little of the later Courtenay, but it is interesting to see how the braced leg of a Courtenay–Doran figure becomes, when provided with an arm re-modelled in a more balanced striking position, the final Courtenay knight. Similarly, a number of his own definitive models display fascinating variations within themselves, achieved either by the different positioning of a limb or a different crest, or the substitution of another rider. Occasionally the fortunate collector may unearth lesser-known models such as the First Guards (1660) suggested to him originally by Ping, but never proceeded with, or crossbowmen in Edward IVs livery, made exclusively for Ping, or the 'Walter Manny' bearing the legend 'Made by Courtenay'.

Some fortunate or prescient collectors purchased their Courtenay models when they were at the original price of 7s 6d; in the course of time they rose to two guineas, and Ionce, as a very young man, saw them in Hummels at a reduced half-price. Before his death the mounted models were £5 to £6 each. It is interesting to note their progress through the recently-formed auction sales dealing exclusively in model soldiers. A few years ago the Courtenay models suffered badly by comparison with Britains, Elastolin and the like. More recently, however, they are gaining the attention they deserve, and are fetching on an average £7 to £8 for a foot figure and up to £25 for a mounted knight.

Although Courtenay is no longer alive, his models are still available. His son, together with Mr Webb of Hummels, had the prescience to hand the moulds over to Frederick Ping. Since they have been in his hands a new Courtenay has emerged. Ping has entirely revolutionised the range, altering the position of a horse, giving it a new rider, providing a different crest, combining different models on one stand in an entirely new way. Models long out of issue are being recast, including the Babylonians and the famous 6in Black Prince. Ping's entirely personal choice of colours and methods of painting is not Courtenay's, but many collectors find the results particularly vibrant. The purists may cavil, the recorders of models find it infuriating, but the students of heraldry are more than satisfied. If, however, the grumblers can accept that there are now two types of Courtenay: the original, and the completely new Courtenay–Ping conception, they will, if they are honest with themselves, admit that Ping has created an entirely satisfying amalgam. He has, as it were, re-created with reverence and integrity, and at the same time provided a seemingly inexhaustible supply of variations on an original theme. Anyone in doubt should pay a visit to Hummels, the only place where they are available, but do not expect to be able to purchase castings. Courtenay–Ping models are only issued painted.

Ping himself was one of the founders of the new school of British makers, and was alone (and still is) in British circles in using continental techniques, for whereas Courtenay and others who will be mentioned cast their models in one piece, Ping builds up his models by solder and sheet-lead on a prototype torso. The result is that no two of his models are ever exactly alike. For some years he was content to assist Courtenay and others, and to remain quietly in the background, but a set of his Scottish clansmen were eagerly seized upon, and he began to make and market models on his own account. He soon began to specialise in the medieval period, and evolved a particular style of his own. His models are couched in a quiescent vein, and have a reticence all too uncommon, especially in these days of furious activity. Gradually he built up a circle of discriminating clients, for whom he executed many commissions. One of the key-notes to his success has been his choice of colours and his application of paint, and also his scrupulous regard for the armour and the heraldry of the period represented. Especially delightful are his costume models, both male and female, and I recall with delight a set he made for Brigadier Young of 'The Beggar's Opera', and collectors will remember the series of stage figures he made for Peter Cushing. After many years of providing delight for discerning collectors, he is now limiting his output to his inherited Courtenay moulds and whatever commission takes his fancy. He will only sell his models painted, and, as with Courtenay, Hummels is his sole agent.

Carrying on the tradition founded by Britains, but this time in solid lead, was the task of John Greenwood. He, like Courtenay, had begun by making commercial 45mm models of medieval subjects, but soon turned his attention to the portrayal of British line regiments, at which he became pre-eminent. His models in this sphere are perhaps the most static and traditional and approach more fully the original conception of the times in which he first operated; for these particular figures he never changed his style. Although the anatomy is excellent, the slightly odd-shaped nose that occurs on all the faces detracts from the complete model, and unfortunately becomes enlarged by photography. His later conceptions of Nazis and his mounted models are not in the same class. At the outset of World War II he began to make the most delightful 20mm models for dioramas, and many of these have found their way all over the world. His original models were painted by Mrs Nathaniel (née Katherine Ball) who did much to ensure his popularity.

Greenwood died in 1971, but his name was taken over by W. F. Pearce, and some of the original models are still obtainable. The painting, following in Miss Ball's tradition, is not of the same quality, and some collectors may find the price of a simple medieval foot-soldier expensive at £3.50.

To complete this quartet of English makers is W. Y. Carman. Interested at an early stage in the possibility of the production of a somewhat better model than was at the time available, he learned casting under the guidance of Courtenay and Ping, and was encouraged by his association with the well-known émigré Otto Gottstein. His initial aim was to produce a series of models of British soldiers in the Waterloo campaign to parallel the famous Mond collection of Lucottes. This idea never fully materialised, however, but Carman produced a number of solid models, which, judged by present-day standards, did not reach the heights, but were of considerable ability and provided welcome variety. These included Elizabethan and Spanish pikemen, and a series of Magna Carta knights which were very popular. Other medieval models were disappointing, except a civilian range which was delightfully colourful. A projected group of cavaliers, made in collaboration with Peter Young, was interrupted by World War II. His association with Gottstein enabled him to learn the intricacies of casting flat figures, and the resultant set of Kings and Queens of England, still outstanding in quality, were the first flats to be made and produced in England. His enthusiasm and historical knowledge, as well as his association with the artists of his day, went far to provide a solid basis for later English makers.

All the makers mentioned above were well established by the outbreak of World War II, and after hostilities had ceased they were joined by a number of others who helped in spreading the interest and in enlarging the field, and who, happily, are with one exception, still flourishing and providing the solid basis of the hobby.

Pre-eminent among them is Charles C. Stadden. In terms of variety and quantity his output can only be regarded as phenomenal. He made a tentative beginning about 1945, and since then he has dominated the scene, becoming a household word. Although the quality of his models is self-evident, he is always improving or remaking earlier models. The market for his productions is now such that he himself only makes the master figure; the casting, the changing of posture ('animating'), the painting and the marketing are executed under the auspices of Norman Newton Ltd (Tradition) of Piccadilly, hence the name erroneously given to his models on many occasions, especially by continental writers. So much has been written about him, and his works so frequently illustrated, that it is difficult to find anything new to say.

What is certain is that he and Roy Belmont-Maitland have between them created an empire of their own, and expanded the model soldier industry far beyond the dreams of Greenwood,

Courtenay or Ping; it would not be questioned that his models form the basis of more collections all over the world than any other maker. Indeed, they were the first English models (apart from the hollow-casts) to be imported into the United States, and when shown first in Germany they created a sensation among the devotees of the first traditional flats.

There appears to be no period that he (and other designers working with him) has not attempted (not always successfully, it must be said), yet he regularly increases his already vast range, and no one catalogue could cover every model he has made or redesigned. Indeed, in years to come this task might well occupy the attention of a student of military models.

Inevitably the Napoleonic period is his most popular, and here collectors are well served. It is covered in such detail as to dominate the field until the arrival of Historex. The French side had always been obtainable in France, but Stadden was the first maker to really attempt a representative showing of the British at Waterloo, and it is obvious that he takes great delight in his portrayal of the British infantryman who fought in that campaign and also in the Peninsular War.

'Tradition' 's *Model Soldiers*, dealing entirely with Stadden's work, and covering a mere tenth of it, is divided chronologically. First, a glimpse at Rome – Stadden has made far more than those illustrated. Next, the Middle Ages – distinguished knights, some mounted (these are disproportionately expensive) others on foot, the elaborate painting and the rich armorial bearings not concealing a certain top-heaviness. Variations on a few basic stances are achieved by the use of different weapons and helms. Then follows in quick succession the army of Frederick the Great, the American War of Independence, and the Napoleonic wars (the standards are particularly attractive). Succeeded by the Austrian Army 1813–1914, the Franco-Prussian War, the British Army 1825–1914, the Indian Army 1910 (including the Camel Corps), the German Army 1900–14, the Russians 1911–14, and World War I.

For sheer bulk this is staggering, and one can forgive the

occasional unfelicitous horse. Emphasised by the photographs in the book quoted, the more recent bulk-style of painting, with quite unnecessary and tasteless heavy lining down the sides of the mouth and the nose, and the oblong, doll-like eyes, is not to everybody's taste, and compares unfavourably with the early specimens that may be seen at Blenheim Palace. This is not so evident in the unillustrated ranges that Stadden makes so beautifully: that of the two extremes, 30mm and 90mm. If one likes small models, the former should satisfy the most discriminating; if the statuette-type, the latter are outstanding in their field.

Stadden's models are issued either animated, unpainted or painted, or in kit form. Certain of them are to be found under the 'Tradition' name-ranges – 'Tradition', 'Standish', and 'Just Soldiers'. He is also the designer of Minimodels (45mm plastic) and Almark (54mm and 25mm). The size of the later Stadden models is nearer 56–8mm, and they do not always fit in easily with those of other makers.

In 1953 there appeared a set of models commemorating the Coronation of Queen Elizabeth II. They were issued under the name of Graham Farish, but enquiries revealed that they were the work of Russell Gammage. The characteristics of the models were sensibility, grace and impeccable craftsmanship. Although his models, marketed under the name of 'Rose', are now also collected throughout the world, he still maintains the high standards set by these early ones. He is one of the few makers working within his own capacities. One imagines that he does not aspire to set the world on fire, but to provide a genial and glowing warmth. The result is that one hardly ever comes across an unworthy model, and his 54mm scale is always correct. His models are in a sense traditional, in that they generally display a refreshing calmness of pose in a world of violent animation. Yet he is by no means bound to one period, but roams freely over history, from Greece, Rome and Egypt to World War II, with no particular concentration on any, appearing to be equally at home in all. Probably his

Romans have the most immediate effect, but many collectors are proud to possess his Indian Army troops and his county regiments. As a collector interested primarily in the Middle Ages, I have always regretted that his offerings in this field are severely restricted, but most acceptable none the less; perhaps he will one day reward us by a whole series. He is particularly happy with Egyptians, both male and female, and his Ptolemaic chariot is a delight. It seems all the more regrettable that he should depict Boadicea being thrashed by her Roman captors.

Gammage was one of the first in the field with his wargame models, and also an early pioneer in the issuing of models in unassembled form. He also supplies a whole host of separate heads which inevitably become transplanted to another body, even of an alien material. The only critical note one might venture to make is to suggest that the size and anatomy of one or two horses' heads of later periods are not quite up to Gammage's high standard, but no doubt these will be remade in due course.

When the models of Marcus Hinton (Hinton-Hunt) appeared first in 1957, they did not attract immediate attention, and it has been by sheer tenacity and improved technique that they have now reached their present popularity. He covers the Napoleonic period in depth, and a number of otherwise rarely depicted units appear in his list. His medieval collection is interesting more for its individual treatment of different periods of armour than for its overall excellence. Good, sound workmanship is evident, and care has been taken to ensure that the heraldry is of the correct date, but the models themselves are somewhat lifeless. The exceptions are the archer, with his sharpened stake, the crossbowman with his pavisse, and the mounted range, including a fine Joan of Arc. He also makes a long range of Crimean War figures with more success, and the American Revolutionary War series is figured strongly in catalogues from dealers in the United States. He is constantly adding fresh periods, and has at times a welcome sense of the ridiculous which adds greatly to the appeal of a model. The accessories such as rifle racks, strips of pavé, gabions, and the like, are most useful to makers of dioramas, and he continues to issue vast quantities of wargame figures.

In general, although the majority of Hinton's models (even the mounted ones) do not quite reach the heights of craftsmanship, the solid core that they provide is most satisfying, and overall they form a worthy contribution, although, again, the size is roughly that of 56–8mm. He has recently partially accepted the current method of presentation, and certain of his medieval and Napoleonic models are obtainable in kit form under the name of 'Guard House'.

The first really fine model that I ever possessed was a delightful 20mm mounted knight made by John Niblett, given to me by Mr C. Webb, the proprietor of Hummels. In the course of time I met the maker himself, and received from him a little batch of foot-knights and figures depicting the English Civil War. These lovely little figures were the first to be made in England in such a tiny size, and they remain the finest in this particular scale. Niblett had previously made 54mm models of the medieval period, but these 'tinies' took the collector's imagination. Later Niblett took over the designing of models for Airfix, and concentrated on their 20mm wargame plastic models.

At the other end of the scale Sentry Box issued very large models of infantry and cavalry units of the British Army. Beginning in 1950 with these models in a plaster composition, they gradually evolved a method of cupronising them, until within the last few years they have completely redesigned the whole series and brought out further models, all of them in metal. They come within the scope of presentation figures, except for a limited range of portrait models in 54mm, which are available unpainted. For display in a case or under a glass dome the larger models are ideal, and the painting is most sensitive and accurate. They are obtainable in kit form or assembled, direct from the designer or from Hummels.

Page 33 (*above*) Germanic solids: a group of models, various scales, of the British Army c1900 by George Heyde, the most prolific of the German makers of solids; (*below*) The famous models of the first British commercial manufacturer, William Britain, still command the respect of a dedicated group of collectors. Armoured car; Devon and Dorset Regiment; Russian Infantry, Australian Infantry; Queen's Company of Archers; ski troops; Home Guard; US Infantry; British staff officer; Life Guard.

Page 34 (*above*) Josianne Desfontaines is one of the two finest contemporary makers of model-soldiers, the other being Roger Berdou. This group displays her varied art at its best. The war-elephant scene took two years to complete. The owner, Nathan Polk, is in the background; (*below*) Probably the best-known name in the model-soldier world, Charles C. Stadden, covers the whole range of history. This group is typical of his work in 56mm.

3

THE NEW MEN

While the old-established model-makers were perfecting the technique acquired after years of experience and experiment, and widening the scope of their products, a new school was gradually emerging, bringing with it a new impetus and fresh methods of production. With the complete and utter passing of the hollow-cast, the field was wide open, the choice lying between the solid individual model and the alkathene and polystyrene plastic invasion.

Stadden, Gammage, Greenwood and Hinton had shown the way, and the newcomers had sound foundations to build upon. The most outstanding difference that emerged was in the method of marketing. The economic situation was responsible to a large degree. Whereas the established makers had been able to set up studios and employ technicians and painters, the new men just did not have the necessary capital for this, and consequently they had to limit their workforce. Again, the wish of many collectors to assemble and to paint their models themselves had been growing, and this, of course, made production cheaper. As has been mentioned, Stadden and Gammage had to a limited degree fitted in with these wishes, at the same time maintaining their assembly and paint shops for such clients who still desired an animated or painted model, and for despatching models to agents for display.

So the new aspect of the model was to assume the following forms:

1 Unassembled, in untouched metal, sold in a plastic or cellophane envelope or box
2 Assembled and/or undercoated
3 Assembled and painted

And all three stages can be seen in most modern hobby stores.

The new men, therefore, when advertising, priced their models as either in kit form or painted. It is obvious that the assembled and painted model would have undergone the necessary refinements before it was placed on sale, but the onus still remained on the maker to ensure that all parts of his unassembled kit were free from 'flash' (extraneous metal), that footpegs protruding from the base were removed, and all parts fitted well together. (Unfortunately in practice, this is not always carried out, and some of the makers of wargame models are particularly neglectful.) A further extension followed. The established makers, although they might cast the head, legs, arms and weapons of their models in separate moulds, would still, if required, assemble them to the torso and peg the legs to the footstands. To achieve variety of posture, or 'animate' the figure, they changed the direction of a head, or raised or lowered an arm. Now, suddenly, the customer was left to do this. Normally this is an admirable practice, as it allows the collector to achieve whatever pose he desires, but if the neck shaft is minutely too large for its socket, or the peg of the arm too short, or the stubs of the feet are protruding, then frustrating filing and the use of plugging material is necessary. I recently received a 40mm mounted model where the pegs under the feet had not been removed. On such a tiny figure the threat of damage to the adjacent spurs was quite considerable, and it was only with great difficulty that they were eventually removed. Furthermore, the lance was in two badly joined sections of spindly copper wire. I felt that for the £1 I had paid a better finished model should have arrived. Not all the new makers, however, abandoned the old methods, as will be discovered.

Edward Surén (Willie Figures) is a traditionalist. All his

work displays great elegance, and he has a fine grasp of equine anatomy. From a slow and tentative beginning in 1964 the quality of his models and the entrancing 30mm size that he favours has now assured him of a place among the most talented makers, and his range has greatly increased. The eighteenth century was his first love, and the beauty of these models comes home forcibly when they are seen *en masse*. But they may also be displayed to equal advantage either singly or in small groups, to be studied for their own inherent qualities. It would be difficult to select any particular series for special mention – each collector will have his own personal favourite, whether it be the Romans, Normans and Saxons, the Queen Anne and Georgian period, the Napoleonic campaigns, the Crimean or the Franco-Prussian wars, or the South African troops.

Surén is turning more and more to the production of dioramas, and has achieved notable successes with those of Ticonderoga, Rorke's Drift and Quatre Bras, whilst the colour photography of Philip Stearns has introduced his models to a wide and appreciative audience. Within my own particularly favoured period there is a fine mounted Richard I and a knight in Maximilian armour (the horse is disappointing, with neither armour nor trappings). There are a further two knights, caparisoned and emblazoned in colours and gold, which I saw in Surén's shop, and which do not at the time of writing appear in his catalogue. I was told that they were seldom cast, and then only by special request. This is not surprising, perhaps, when they cost four or five times as much as Eriksson's comparable models. If they were reduced in price, it seems certain that they would be assured of a fantastic sale.

Surén has also made a range of 60mm semi-nude females, the purpose of which escapes me, beautiful though they are. More understandable is his fine chess-set of the rival troops at the Battle of Pavia. Here the pawns and the castles are in 30mm, the bishops and knights 40mm, and the kings and queens 54mm. The set is issued painted only, at £150 in an edition limited to twenty-five sets.

Another exponent of the smaller-sized model was Leslie Higgins, whose premature death in 1972 cut short a highly promising career. He began with exquisite 25mm models, beautifully painted, of Royalist and Cromwellian troops, very similar to those made by Niblett. The range was expanded to include cavalry, with the riders cast separately, and to these were added the Marlborough period. Models in 30mm of the ancient world, the Napoleonic wars and the Sudan expedition followed, and Higgins also designed a series of British line regiments (with bandsmen), Highland and Lowland pipes and drums, Greeks, and the English Civil War.

An impressive group in 56mm followed, including Royalist and Cromwellian pikemen and officers, a dismounted dragoon, an ensign with flag, and a cavalry officer preaching from the saddle. These are still obtainable (unpainted) from Phoenix Model Developments (B. L. Marlow), who took over Higgins's moulds, and who has added considerably to the existing lines. He now employs a number of designers, of whom the principal is T. C. Richards, who has made a remarkable kit of 'Young Winston'. Marlow himself has made an RAF pilot.

An execrable Hitler was probably the worst figure Higgins ever made. A 30mm range of the Civil War, including a girl camp-follower, was marketed under the name of 'Jason', and he made a most attractive series of 56mm models especially for Norman Newton Ltd, originally entitled 'Pagana', and now included in the 'Tradition' range. These were of Elizabeth I, Henry VII, Henry VIII, Lady Jane Grey and an executioner, a burgomaster, and a regency couple. One of the most pleasing models that I possess is a Samuel Pepys which Higgins gave me, and he also produced an amusing series of Dickens characters, and a powder-monkey of great character. In general it is possible that in the larger size models some might find a number of the faces a little ill-designed, and the fingers rather shapeless, but by and large Higgins's models have character and originality.

Upon Greenwood's death, a friend of long-standing, W. F.

Pearce, acquired the moulds, and immediately began to recast models from them. At the same time he seized the opportunity of commissioning models of other styles and periods, issued under the all-embracing Greenwood & Ball title. The subdivisions are: Lasset (John Tassell), Minot (Barry Minot), Olive (R. J. Marrion), Garrison (John Braithwaite) and Sanderson (Cliff Sanderson). Together they form a solid block of models obtainable from the same source.

John Tassell began creating 54mm models about 1972. His range is gradually increasing, and includes small groups of Napoleonics and troops from Hesse-Darmstadt, as well as a most unusual collection of native tribesmen for the Omdurman campaign (including a Taaislie warrior of the Baggara tribe riding a camel, and a mounted Emir of the Khalifa's bodyguard), and a representative clutch of German, British, American and Russian troops of World War II (including paratroops and ski-units, and a mounted Cossack). Added to these is a two-man machine-gun crew behind a wall. He also makes models of Baylor's Dragoons and Rogers' Rangers of the American War of Independence, together with an Indian scout and an American rifleman. Latest additions are a fine series of Romans (some mounted) and medieval knights from the Normans onwards. His work is distinguished by its clarity of execution and its lack of bombast. At one time associated with Norman Newton, for whom he constructed dioramas and designed some models, and with Series 77 at its birth, he is now working entirely in 54mm.

Barry Minot has as yet only a small offering consisting of the Napoleonic period. It comprises the Emperor himself, officer, trumpeter, trooper, and chasseur à cheval, and also includes the Hussar Élite Company with busby, in parade dress and on campaign, as well as a British and Highland infantryman and fusilier which unfortunately lack character. In April 1973 he joined the makers of 30mm models with a remarkable series of the British Army at Waterloo, including a specially fine group on one stand, depicting amongst others a wounded figure.

Then in 1974 he not only broke away from Greenwood & Ball, but produced his first 54mm models.

Cliff Sanderson first attracted attention with a set of a Roman slave auction, which was refreshingly unmilitary in character. The figures are full of character but not very well cast, to these has been added a tavern wench or two. This range was followed by a series of studies of girls wearing helmets or boots of various periods – and nothing else. Far more conventional are his gladiators, full of action and purpose, and, according to the experts, historically accurate in their armour and accoutrements, and some outstanding Commonwealth gallants. Of a further venture, this time in nude figures, the least said the better.

R. J. Marrion was well known in collecting circles and had indeed made a few models for giving away before he linked up with Pearce to produce his Olive series. An as yet small range comprises a group of British and Boer representatives, a trooper of the Guards Camel Corps, a Zulu War lancer and infantryman, cavalry from the Egyptian and Second Afghan Wars, and an infantryman in shirt sleeves and braces. Unusual figures to complete the collection are those of a US Cavalry trooper, an Indian scout, and a French hussar in stable dress. All are dismounted, and well designed.

The final maker in the school is John Braithwaite, who is responsible for a 54mm Roman, marketed under the name of Greenwood & Ball, and for a remarkable series of wargame models which will be discussed under the appropriate chapter.

Cliff Sanderson's name crops up again, under the lightly veiled pseudonym 'Saunderson', in a collaboration with John Barber in the production for A. Robinson (Model Figures and Hobbies) of a series entitled Jackboot. Beautifully proportioned, and shallowly though adequately detailed, they are mainly of the Nazi army, including an officer with a map, and a private with a guard dog. A return is made to World War I with an infantryman, appropriately stout, with stein in hand. A breakaway is the 'Trumpeter of the Hillsborough Guard', an elegant and colourful model. Jackboot models are a genuine 54mm size, with simply moulded but expressively individual faces.

J. A. Collins and W. A. Collins (Jac Models) have produced an impressive collection. So far they have made some fifty-odd specimens of the Napoleonic period, including French grenadiers, chasseurs à pied, fusiliers, flanquers, and voltiguers; British infantry, fusiliers, dragoons, riflemen, and Royal Scots Greys (dismounted), together with a few representatives from Austria, Bavaria, Spain, and Italy. Featured also are British troops 1730–50, British infantry 1878–1900, a mounted Roundhead trooper, and a Luftwaffe paratrooper.

As important is their collection of medieval fighting men. A swiftly growing output features troops both on foot and mounted. The horses are really strong destriers, in fairly quiescent action apart from one rearing specimen. The riders, who are cast separately, exhibit careful portrayal of physiognomy, one in particular, bareheaded, with helm in hand, is a most unusual figure. The footmen and the crossbowmen display a curious disregard for anatomy, appearing much too tall and flat for their bulk, resulting in a certain pigeon-chested and spindle-legged appearance. However, the armour is well done, and the makers have looked for a refreshing originality of treatment.

Well known to individual members of societies, but not so much to the general model-buying public, is the work of Anthony Fermor (Frontier). He is a retiring man, which is probably one of the reasons why his models are not more widely known. He is almost unique in that his career began when he asked his friends the style and period of history that they required, and then made a model to accommodate them. The result is a series of figures not apparently conforming to any set pattern, which is refreshing. The earliest time represented in Fermor's list is an Etruscan warrior, then a Celtic man with a spear. A series of English sovereigns follows: Edward the Confessor, Harold, William I, Richard I, John, Richard II in coronation robes, Richard III, Henry VIII, Elizabeth I, and Victoria, enthroned. Other figures of these periods are of a Plantagenet noble, Joan of Arc (in hose and doublet, holding a cross, with attendant English soldiers), the boy princes, linked together on one stand, an executioner with the block, the Earl of Leicester and Sir Walter Raleigh. Other civilian models are of Florence Nightingale, Mata Hari, a Hanoverian noble, a lady in a sedan chair with two bearers and a link boy with a torch.

The British Army is represented by single figures of a musketeer of 1660, a grenadier of the 20th Foot and an 11th Dragoon (both 1759), a 2nd Foot officer (1821), Infantry of the 89th Foot and 11th Hussars (both 1854), a Royal Engineers officer (1874), and various units of World War I. To show that Mr Fermor is alive to collectors' requirements, he has designed a Heavy Dragoon and a British Hussar (both of 1900) to be used in conjunction with a Historex horse. Nazis, eighteenth- and nineteenth-century Frenchmen, New Zealand Canterbury Volunteers, 60th Canadian (1780), New South Wales Lancer (1900) a Niger Hausa infantry private (1891) and a Jordan desert patrol indicate some of the range, which is constantly expanding.

The models are all in the true 54mm size, and well designed and cast. One or two of them appear a little dumpy about the legs, and the join of the arm at the shoulder is a little indefinite, but the medieval range is certainly delightful, and displays great imagination.

Major Robert Rowe assisted Norman Newton Ltd as an animator for some years, and was responsible for the remarkable series of dioramas incorporating Stadden's models at Woburn Abbey, before he turned to the marketing of his own very fine figures, in a series of about twenty. These included such unusual ones as a US Medical Department Officer (Cuba Campaign 1898), several French Cuirassiers and Hussars *en tenue d'écurie* (1804–12, derived from Rousselot), a FANY officer (1918), a British tank driver (1917) with chainmail face mask, and a Polish Krakusi trooper and officer.

This series became unobtainable about the end of 1972, and Major Rowe and his son were next heard of designing an impressive collection for Vallance in the United States. In the summer of 1973 I received a visit from an old Dutch collector-friend, and at breakfast we were bemoaning the preponderance of Napoleonic and Nazi models which were flooding the market. Then the postman arrived, delivering a set of the Vallance models, and a box containing three remarkable figures. They turned out to be the first of a new series by Rowe, entitled 'Ensign Miniatures', and they proved to be something quite different. The series when complete will consist of twenty figures of British Army officers in mess dress, c1900, in different casual poses and covering all regiments and corps. So casual were the poses that some were without a footstand, and a bench, table or chair was required. Not only were they beautifully sculpted, but the whole idea was most refreshing.

A diversity of models is evident in the work of W. Kirk. The mounted ones comprise such subjects as 6th Dragoon officers (1808–10), 1st Dragoon officers (1879), 17th Lancers and Hussars, Polish Lancer troopers and trumpeters, and the Black Prince. The unmounted models include Simon de Montfort and a Viking, Henry VIII, Oliver Cromwell, Bonnie Prince Charlie, Wellington, Napoleon and other representatives of that era, including an able seaman and Hussars of 1854. An unusual model is that of General Bolivar's bodyguard. The Black Prince is in 60mm, and some collectors may not be happy with the use of steel wire for the tail and plasticard for the bridle-mountings, the engraved heraldry is rather coarse, and the oversize quasi-banner heraldically incorrect.

Michael R. John once operated under two names: Trophy and Harlech. They are now combined under the former. Outstanding is a mounted knight (58mm) on a sturdy horse, equipped with lance and sword, with a choice of three detachable helms. The removable stirrups are of copper, and sheet lead is provided for the making of a banner. Unfortunately the alignment of the two pieces of the horse was not accurate in the model I received, which entailed hours of adjustment and filing, hardly expected at the rather high price at which the model sells. Other figures include a splendid and elaborate Samurai mounted archer (sold with base scenery), George Washington and an English bowman. John's greatest admirer would hardly call his Murat a success, but two Napoleonic infantrymen, defeated by the Russian winter, are at least unusual.

William Lamming issues his models in spread-eagle torso form; the metal is malleable if gently warmed, thus enabling the collector to animate with little difficulty. Of the ubiquitous Napoleonic period, spare heads and equipment can also be obtained.

John D. Johnston (Douglas Miniatures) began making miniatures for his own pleasure in 1967, and gradually drifted into the regular trade. In strict 54mm size, he issues a clansman and a Royal Fusilier (1689), a Mahadi warrior (1883), an Aztec, a Russian Guard Grenadier (1800), a Spanish Infantry Death Regiment (1808), a British Pikeman (1540), a few mid-nineteenth-century troops, and a sprinkling of the combatants of World War I and II, together with a fair range of wargame models for the Marlburian, Cromwellian, and Napoleonic wars. His models are pleasant, and it is to be hoped that he will in the course of time expand his range.

Frank Hinchcliffe began his career with the making of 54mm artillery, intended for grouping with figures by other makers, as evinced by Gammage's catalogue. From this he proceeded to wargame figures, and, by a logical progression, to the horses and men for his artillery. So that today one can obtain not only a large range of weapons, all most beautifully constructed and cast, but also horse teams for the Napoleonic wars and World War I. All horses are supplied with chains, reins, and traces, together with a splendid set of men for each.

Almark has made a beginning with 54mm metal British infantrymen of World War II, doubtless to be followed by

Germans, Japanese, Americans and Russians. They are in kit form, and of excellent quality.

It might be useful to conclude this chapter by mentioning one or two curiosities connected with many of the models, of prime interest is the reluctance of a number of designers to market some of their models under their own name, making it an infuriating business to try and discover who is responsible for them. In this connection it is pertinent to note that Stadden's models are obtainable in the normal range under his own name (the chief agency is Norman Newton Ltd), as 'Standish' (the earlier models are re-issued in kit form), as 'Tradition' (incorporating models by other designers such as Higgins), and as 'Just Soldiers', a cheaper range. In a similar way, Hinton issues a certain selection of his Napoleonic and medieval models under the name 'Guard House' in which case they cost half the price of their assembled counterparts. It has already been stated that the Roman figure by Greenwood & Ball is in fact designed by Braithwaite, and when the models of the American makers are discussed it will be found that such confusion is even more rampant.

A further curiosity is noted by an American dealer, an editor of a house-journal which he publishes, when he discusses the matter of 'spin-off'. This is the term used to describe figures in which the torso and basic position are essentially the same if not identical to other figures either in the same batch or issued previously, the only differences being a change of head, arm position, or weapon. In some cases the better makers can conceal this so effectively that virtually a new figure emerges, but there are many who cannot do this. The result may well be that a collector, ordering 'blind' from a catalogue, may receive a parcel of half a dozen models all in practically identical poses. This is acceptable if he is thinking in terms of representative uniform, but not so much if he wishes to have an assembly of differently positioned models. There should therefore always be an agreement that the purchaser should have the freedom of returning any such models to the maker. It should be noted that this is no new practice, and applies equally to the makers of most countries.

The reader should also be warned that the 54mm scale is by no means adhered to, indeed, many of the models produced today are tending more to 56 or even 58mm.

4

THE UNITED STATES

In the United States the story is of an ever-expanding industry. From the early days of the century, when McLoughlin was turning out solids of the Heyde type, to the amalgamation of Imrie and Risley, there has been a native school of makers of both solids and hollow-casts. The professionals covered a wide range with their productions, with the emphasis mainly on the two major American wars. Such firms as the Warren Company, Comet, Lincoln Logs, Military Miniatures, Moulded Miniatures, American Metal Figures, Tru-Craft, Minifigure, Historical Miniatures and Bussler were predominant, whilst Scruby, and later Cox and Thomas, were among the earliest to make 20mm wargame models (Scruby is still active, with 54mm models also, and Thomas's models are still available through Leslie Pierce of K & L Company).

Many of the models produced during the days just before and after World War II were of good quality, and well worthy of collection. The regular makers at that time were supported by a host of gifted 'amateurs': collectors and historians, such as Michael Hitrovo, Custer, the Harles, Scheid, Greer, Conley and Mrs West, who, whilst collecting and welcoming the products of the commerial firms, both native, and European, were at the same time increasingly influenced by the importation of fine European models towards an improved standard in home production. They looked at their Berdous, their des Fontaines and their Courtenays, and realised that they had no makers of the same quality. Their efforts soon began to bear fruit.

The first sign of raised sights was evident about 1956 in the work of William H. Murray and William Imrie. Murray had assistance from Custer and Greer, and began with medieval models of no great quality, and Romans, which were better. He then switched to a long series of the Russian Army of 1812. More recently he has been expanding his range, which includes more recent troops, some by other designers such as Chernak under the name of 'Old Guard'. His models were first conceived in kit form, and they still remain in this manner.

William Imrie began with a series entitled 'Hellenic Miniatures', and has gradually redesigned all of these and added many new models over the course of the years. Today he embraces many periods, from the Middle Ages to World War II. Especially notable are his Napoleonic, American Revolution and Civil War models, in infinite variety, both foot and mounted, and in a great variety of postures. His masterpiece is surely the Revolution cannon with men and heavy draft horses. Specially notable also are his models of the fighting forces of the last war. Since he was joined by Risley the quality has increased, and together they now hold a position in the United States second to none, and comparable to that of Stadden in England. The models are available in kit form, and at reasonable prices. Furthermore, their work is in several other sizes, adding variety to the whole production.

Kaufman (Cockade) produced a notable series of landschnechts and NATO troops, together with an Aztec bearer party, but none of his models have appeared for some years. Norman Cooke (Lance) began well, with the American War of Independence as his prime consideration. He has made some very fine models, including a winged Polish lancer. However, he has been devoting more and more attention to diorama work and specially commissioned figures. Karl M. Ahrens (H.A.M.) began a series of British troops in nineteenth-century full marching order, together with a range of French troops (1806–15) and Germans of World War II, as well as a few models of the ancient world. A firm which no longer appears to be in existence is the Strömbecker Corporation; their catalogue lists sets of models of the War of Independence (cannon and four men), World War I (five Germans and map table), the American Civil War (three foot, one mounted) and American marines in World War II (six action figures). They were not consistently to scale. K-S Miniatures (Kramer and Steiner) made models in 40mm, concentrating on subjects not normally dealt with, such as the Mexican war, the navy in the Civil War, Lexington Light Infantry, Lafayette Escadrilles, and a German U-boat officer.

C. R. Broman (H-R), another of the earlier makers, still flourishing, had made for him by Tom Sibbett some delightful and unconventional figures, especially of Indians, and including a really amusing Mexican generalissimo. More recently he himself has been turning his attention to modern troops, together with 54mm weapons which are in great demand for converting models. A unique figure is that of a US Pilot of World War II, representing himself when stationed in England.

A maker who links the early and later days is William F. Greer, who designed models for Custer and Murray; today he designs for a number of firms, including Monarch and Valiant. Models of his own make, painted by himself and currently available, depict Americans and British of the Revolution, US infantryman (1835–9), Confederates, Charleston S.C. Militia Highland Company (1860), dismounted Plains cavalrymen (1873), clansmen (1715–45), Danish Guard infantry (1777), Olar Rye (killed at Jutland, 1849), and a pilot of World War I. In addition he makes many commissioned models, and is represented at the Old Barracks, Trenton, by a series of dioramas incorporating over two hundred of his own models; he also accepts orders for assembly, conversion and painting. Two of his models are in my collection, and are of outstanding quality.

It has been noted that a number of makers in England issue their models under a nom de guerre. A greater difficulty arises when reviewing American models. In England and on the

Continent most artists work either for themselves or for one agent: thus you usually know where you stand when you purchase a Stadden (even under the name 'Tradition'), or a Surén, or a Ping, or a Gammage (a 'Rose' by any other name!); and even a 'Guard House' discloses itself quite readily. In America, however, one cannot say 'this is by Boutet or Greer, or Paine, or Cade, or Gordon,' because the model you see is issued under the name of a firm, such as Valiant, or Monarch or Aristo-Merité. The cause of this is the number of young men who work 'freelance', and either submit their work to or are commissioned by a corporation. Thus, Valiant has its models designed by as many as eleven artists, making it almost impossible to link the model with its maker. The owner of the firm, Arthur W. Neckermann, tells me that his designers include Sheperd Paine, Ray Anderson, Reginald Boutet, Joe Berton, Ronald Cade, Robert Bihari, William Greer, Frederick Lombardo and Thomas Sibbett, 'plus several who wish to remain anonymous'. To these can be added the name of A. G. Olmstead. Doubts have already begun to arise in America as to whether this is an entirely satisfactory method, especially as a certain amount of plagiarism by contending firms has already undoubtedly arisen.

This use of freelance artists accounts for the dissimilarity of the quality that is to be seen in the products of some firms, especially those of Valiant. The World War II American and British troops are full of life and character, and seem to me to be the best. There is also a very unusual 'Leipzig' series of six models which are quite out of the ordinary. But the 'Barbarian' range is quite another matter. A Nordic warrior with the look of Bruce Bairnsfather's 'Old Bill' does not seem to know quite what to do with his left hand; there is an uninspired El Cid, an anatomically incorrect Viking, a Teutonic chieftain with a curiously shaped nose, a sadistic Vandal, a horrific Visigoth, and an ill-conceived Berserker, and finally a remarkably dull Crusader. Hans Brinker, a Conquistadore, Myles Standish, and a 'young Winston' have a strong element of caricature about

Page 51 (*above*) Medieval nostalgia: the models of Richard Courtenay are eagerly sought after by the connoisseur. Here is a collection of typical examples, including some very rare specimens; (*below*) Chronicle of the Middle Ages: Courtenay and Ping are renowned for their portrayal of the medieval period. In this group the two mounted figures are the Knight and the Squire from *The Canterbury Tales*. These, together with the models of St Louis and his squire, as well as Henry V, were made by Ping especially for the author. The other models are Ping adaptations of Courtenay moulds.

Page 52 (*above*) Traditional: Russell Gammage (Rose Miniatures) has always displayed a high degree of skill and integrity in his 54mm lead models. These British and Scottish soldiers are in the highest tradition of model-making; (*below*) Medieval (mounted): representative works by Imrie-Risley; Kirk (the Black Prince); Jac (including Henry V); Crown Personalities (the Black Prince); Britains; Covington and Trophy.

them, apparently not intended. Outright travesties are Don Quixote and Mr Micawber, whilst the least said of President Nixon the better. Let us have humour by all means, but at the same time the artist has to be skilful. On the credit side, a Gurkha is an imposing figure, and a mounted Mameluke a most imaginative one.

Valiant Miniatures is perhaps typical of the American expansion of the late sixties and early seventies. New makers are appearing as rapidly as in England, and it is virtually impossible to keep pace with them. Nearly all, however, exhibit the same characteristics – a model issued in kit form, and marketed in a plastic envelope, containing a printed card with painting instructions, and on occasions a coloured reproduction of what the completed model should be like. The drawback to this type of packaging is that items of equipment like lances or swords often suffer damage when sent by post. With many of the makers it is difficult to find a connecting theme in the models they issue. Those of Raymond Rubin (Squadron/Rubin) are an example. I have heard of fifty-five so far, and they include such diverse subjects as a Death's Head Hussar, a Confederate cavalry sergeant, a US Cavalry trooper at Wounded Knee, a Mexican Zapata of 1917, a 'Mountie', and several World War II Americans and Germans.

Similarly, a fine series called Aristo-Monogram Merité, discontinued in 1972, but revived the following year, consists of three periods, including a Prussian of 1914, a Luftwaffe paratrooper and other contestants of World War II, a US Green Beret major of 1966, a Viet Cong guerilla, and, of earlier times, Berdan's Sharpshooters and Texas infantry and American infantry of 1780. They are well designed and reasonable in price, although since their re-issue there appears to be a falling-off in the quality of casting. It has also been said that several of the models were originally designed by Reginald Boutet, but this may be open to contradiction.

Boutet certainly was responsible for at least the first six models to be issued by Max Eastman (Cameo), and these must be reckoned as the most accomplished figures yet produced in the United States. The theme is easily discernible: each being a portrait model of a famous modern commander or statesman or personality: Richtofen, Churchill, Hitler, MacArthur, Mussolini, Rommel, and Theodore Roosevelt. A later figure, that of Göering, not designed by Boutet, is also of the highest quality. Certain of the models are being cast in England by Greenwood & Ball.

Another firm with a fairly wide range of interests is Cavalier. The chief designer, Allan Silk, has gathered around him a team consisting of Stackhouse, Chernak, McGerr, Fabre, himself, and, at one time, Rubin. Their World War II models are excellent, especially that of von Runstedt, if one likes this sort of thing. Motorcycle kits and figures are designed by Silk's partner, Edward Lober. Plains Indians and US Cavalry officers complete one of the most capable assemblies of modern times.

Monarch Miniatures also employ a number of designers, including Greer, McGerr, Olmstead, Fabre, and Benkart, and must be the most prolific of producers in the United States, having a representative range from gladiators to the Luftwaffe. However, although employing so many expert designers, the quality of the casting does not do them justice.

Far more attractive are the models emanating from Vallance. The designs are by Major Robert Rowe and his son Robert; each model is a one-piece casting necessitating only the fixing of the weapons. So far they have produced a number of unusual subjects, including a particularly impressive Washington (bearing a remarkable resemblance to Frank Finlay, the actor) Rochambeau, a Rogers' Ranger, a Chiricahua Apache, a most unusual French Dromedary officer and a Russian revolutionary with belted smock-shirt. How refreshing not to have to fix all those arms and legs!

The models associated with the name of D. S. Stewart present the problem of identification mentioned earlier in this chapter. Those of the American Revolution (I have a large batch, kindly sent to me by the owner, William Connolly, of

Waterloo Galleries) are cast in a very soft, malleable lead so that the figures can easily be animated. They are pleasant, but many of the other ranges in this series bear more than the element of caricature about them. The confusion becomes worse when one tries to discover the other parties concerned. A series of US Marines from 1776 to 1847, US Navy and National Period, a clutch of Napoleonics, the two world wars, one or two 'ancients' and a few figures of the Six-Day War, all appear under the embracing name of Waterloo Galleries. However, Connolly informs me that not only Stewart but Beverly Gordon, Chriss Matson, van Tubergen and Connolly himself are responsible for them.

Beverly Gordon, who designed the afore-mentioned Six-Day War camel troops, is working for Scale Specialities Miniatures. The output so far is a line of six models, three German paratroopers and three World War II French soldiers. George van Tubergen, likewise, having recently completed a range of American Civil War naval figures for Waterloo Galleries, is himself making 54 and 30mm models for his own Command Post.

An initial release of five models from TBS (The Barefoot Soldier) are designed by Greer and Cooke. The first three are associated with the struggle between the French Huguenots under René Laudonnière and the Spanish in 1565 for the possession of Florida, and feature a French officer, a Spanish infantryman with arquebus and a Timucua Indian chief. The body paint on the latter is taken from the de Bry engravings. The other models are of a private of the 3rd Louisiana Infantry, and of Waul's Texas Legion (both 1862–3). They are well designed but a little on the large side and unusual in that the hand holding the weapon is moulded with it, and plugs into the arm.

There are many small ventures mushrooming in the United States today. A start obviously has to be made at some time or other, and possibly something great may develop from small beginnings. Edward G. Covington, for example, has to date only three figures for sale: William the Conqueror and a Cuero Dragoon, each in a limited edition of fifty each, and a most spirited Geoffrey de Trumpington which, painted, sells at $150 (£58). Further pieces are to include a companion knight and a Robin Hood set. Mike Ferguson (Soldiers Unlimited) issues a small range (some designed by Richard Kramer), supplied in kit form, of a group of five Assyrians and Persians, a Royal Marine Light Infantry officer and a Royal Engineer officer (both 1900), a British Hussar (1880), and a set of three native gunners plus a British NCO of the Madras Foot Artillery (1845). He plans to add the Indian Army line infantry from 1757 to the Mutiny.

William C. Shotts (Scrimshander) has so far only produced a Texas Ranger and Jim Bridger, the scout and buffalo hunter, but a number of other models he has made have not yet appeared at the time of writing; whilst Dr Alan C. Scott has produced a Roman aquilifier and a Texas infantry sergeant (1839). Donald Polland specialises in the portrayal of the Indian, commencing some years ago with Military Miniatures, he is equally at home with either bronze or lead in 60mm, as can be seen in his action-filled group in bronze of three cowboys representing the personification of Remington. The smaller size of 30mm has new adherents in Tom Bookwalter and Stanley Glanzer (Bugle & Guidon), producing Indians and US Cavalry (as well as a few 54mm models), in Stan Johansen (formerly Victory Miniatures) who makes Napoleonic troops, the American War of Independence, and a range of foot and mounted Samurai, and lastly in GHQ, who produce models and vehicles of all periods.

Finally, mention must be made of a range of what would normally be regarded as souvenirs but at the same time are of great interest to collectors of model soldiers. They are designed by Norman Cooke, and produced by K/S Pewter Miniatures (Robert Kammer) and deal with the American War of Independence.

5

EUROPE

As far as lead models are concerned the practice in France is the exact reverse of that of the United States. The former relies almost entirely on the works of her master-makers, who are commissioned by individual clients, and there are no makers with large lists such as Imrie-Risley or Stadden in England. Mignot are the only firm of commercial manufacturers in lead, and they still command a high respect in their own country. A year or two ago they circulated to certain dealers in England lists of selected models, but nothing ever materialised, because they changed their minds and confined their attention to the United States.

As an indication of the prices they expected, boxes of four infantrymen would have cost £7 ($18), of eight £13.50 ($35), and of twelve £19.70 ($50). Drummers and bandsmen were priced even higher.

In Germany flats are still of prime importance, and little interest is taken in the solid model. In Austria, however, there is still a following for the archaic 35 and 54mm semi-solids of the prolific Kober, whilst Uwe Lacina has been specialising in splendid 30mm models of eighteenth-century troops.

Spain, on the other hand, is much more enterprising. The tradition of the solid model began with Casanellas some eighty years ago, and continued with Palomeque, even though both these makers turned out some extremely queer models anatomically. The most prolific of modern makers is José Almirall. He has a long list of Napoleon's troops, both foot and mounted, including portraits of the marshalls. In the same period are the Allies, with a predominance of Russians. The Spanish are represented strongly, as is to be expected, in most periods up to the Civil War. There is also a group of artillery, and an unusual and effective sideline is a set of the kings and queens of Spain from Ferdinand V to Alfonso XIII. Almirall is modest, and does not claim that his models are anything other than pedestrian. However, they are more varied than Britains, and the painting is adequate. During the last few years his models have improved in quality, especially his horses, of which those for artillery are monumental specimens. Some collectors may feel that he is underestimating his own ability, for his models have proved extremely popular in Canada, the United States and Australia, and one Dutch collector must have accumulated a complete set of everything Almirall has made. (Not Aylmer, as stated in *Model Soldiers for the Connoisseur*, p. 207.)

Lucio Saez-Alcocer, similarly, issues a large number of models (he himself says in the region of 5,000) in 30, 45 and 54mm, both foot and mounted, together with artillery. The larger models are of good quality, and are sold painted. So also are those in 45mm, whilst the 30mm are made as castings only. Each size covers a wide range, and of the 45mm the Napoleonic period is outstanding. The smallest size features in particular the Indian wars of 1754–63.

Troops of the Third Reich are a speciality of José M. Alarcon (Soldat, formerly Franco). Designed by Ramon Casadevall, so far they number about thirty, including the Afrika Corps, paratroopers and standard bearers. The models are well sculpted and painted. When the German units have been completed they will be followed by troops of other nations. They will be obtainable through several agents in England.

Appearing in London and New York from time to time are the remarkable 20mm 'Miniploms' of Angel Comes Placencia (Alymer) which disappear just as regularly. Their sixty-page catalogue (illustrated in colour) lists over twenty-seven different periods from antiquity to 1940. The infantry are sold in boxes of two or three figures, the cavalry in ones or twos, and there are also such items as a series of chariots, a war-elephant, artillery, and carriages of different eras. They are at first sight most attractive, although the infantry are all in the same marching position. The cavalrymen, however, are more varied, as are the ancient races. The prime objection to them is their prohibitive price when imported.

Less well known are their larger models, which to my knowledge have never been seen in England but are available in New York. A 33mm range follows more or less the content of the smaller one, but with much more variety in posture. Different nations, however, are often simple repaints. There appear to be six basic designs for the horses. The chariots are fascinating. In 54mm size there is a large group of ancient races, there being two or three figures for each particular country or tribe, all of which are different, ranging from ancient Egypt to the Anglo-Saxons. They are all extremely colourful, and include such lesser-known tribes as the Phrygians, the Scythians, the Philistines, and the Canaanites. They also make a short series of troops of 1940 and 1970.

The models of Vicente Julia Manuel, covering Spain (1808–12, 1872–6, and 1936–9), are very good commercial specimens, well painted, and with individual physiognomy. Personalities include José Antonia, General Franco, Valentin Gonzalez, and General Mola. Numerous collections in Spain also contain the models of Echeverria and of Solana, both of whom have given up production.

Some of the most outstanding models however are made by Ramon Labayen. I have one of Marshal Berthier, holding a baton and sword. The gold decoration on the uniform, the braid, sash and the froggings are incredibly well painted. Alas, the eyes are over-emphasised. Labayen has four series in being, all of the Napoleonic era, including the whole of Napoleon's staff. He is also projecting a range of the French during the American Revolution. The models are sold either as castings, or in 'standard painting' or in 'master painting'. Any model not up to the designer's standard is removed from the market. He acknowledges his early indebtedness to the Stadden models he saw whilst in London in 1961, and has obviously been influenced by them.

In Italy a firm that is still resisting the plastic wave by continuing to make its models in metal is I.S.A. (Industria Soprammobili Artistici) of Turin, founded in 1954, and marketed by the Pelli-Cini family. A large range is available, the quality being somewhat similar to Britain's later competitors. An older firm, Antonini (1927) covers every branch of Italian military history. Here the riders are detachable, but the models have a doll-like appearance. However, they are still extremely popular in their own country, and can be seen in large quantities in the Nelli and the Testi collections.

There are also one or two semi-private makers of models in 54mm, of whom Amanzio Bormioli producing Piedmontese army types may be taken as a typical example.

The Scandinavian countries have no mass-producers; instead, they rely on traditional flats and semi-flats, with a few specialist makers for variation. In Sweden the best-known and oldest established is Holger Eriksson. The discerning collector goes to him. He has not confined himself to his own freelance production, however; he was active in the design of the Comet-Authenticast models and those of S.A.E., whose casting was not worthy of his designs. He is also responsible for the originals for the moulds of a self-casting set issued by Jan Edman of Vagnharad.

Magnus Schreiber, an ex-naval officer, began making models about five years ago, as a hobby, and continues to do so without any commercial interests. He makes about ten copies of each, simply for distribution to friends, and, as his interest is purely in their construction, he keeps few for himself. Confined mainly to the 1790–1813 period, his models are full of life, of an enviable quality, and beautifully painted.

The Dane Søren Brunoe (Rollo) is making a name for himself with his delightful 54mm models. He happily seems to find equal interest in the making of female figures, which fit most artistically into his own rococo settings. Indeed, he is turning more and more to large scale diorama work. His military subjects can be seen in England, but it may be that they are a little expensive for the collector who has been drugged by cheaper prices and less imaginative conceptions.

J. Johanssen and R. Anholm have given delight for years to Danish collectors, and more recently John Buntzen has been concentrating on the British Overseas Army, making his own elephants and camels (which he will sell if requested), whilst Ole Høyer has joined J. W. Hansen in the production of a series of 54mm models of Swedish historical troops, of which the former designs the figures and the latter casts and produces them, and both do the painting.

In general Europe has remained attached to the traditional model. Belgium certainly has collectors for their own MIM, made by Andersen about the mid-sixties, but although there are quite a number of enthusiasts in the Low Countries who make their own models, they are not interested in marketing them. On the other hand, British, American and Spanish models appear regularly in the shops both here and in Scandinavia, together with flats and plastics of all kinds, whilst Historex kits are as popular as in other countries.

6

THE SMALL AND THE LARGE

One of the aspects of the model-soldier world which has progressed to an incredible degree is the wargame. Its origins go back to the middle of the nineteenth century, when, in Germany, as 'kriegspiel' it was regarded as a necessary adjunct to professional military training. It was introduced to the non-military public in England in a modified and play-like form by H. G. Wells just before World War I, and continued in this primitive and not over-taxing way until about the middle of the 1930s. It would be difficult to say how and when a more sophisticated approach was made. It grew probably from an interchange of ideas between collectors rather than from a formal 'declaration of war'. The modern versions are legion, and have been so thoroughly examined by so many experts that there is no point in pursuing it further, apart from looking at the models used in its pursuit.

This is an age in which the thought of war is abhorrent to many. The endless massacres that occur in Africa, the holocaust of the Vietnamese conflict, the savagery of the fratricidal struggle in Northern Ireland, all extensively reported in the press, all brought visually nearer by television, have sickened many people, and caused them to question the validity of settling problems by armed combat. However, and seemingly paradoxically, never has there been such a welter of books concerning war, especially World War II, and never have they had such an enthusiastic reception. Equally there have never been so many volumes dealing with uniforms, tanks and weapons; even the most bestial of armies is treated in depth, and instruments of destruction made available in replica.

World War I began in a spirit of patriotism, reflected by the poets who, whilst recognising its terrible implications, could yet see some reason for it. The last war, on the other hand, was fought with a grim realisation that it was a job that had to be done, and, when finished, best forgotten. Thirty years is, of course, a long time to remember, and perhaps as time goes on, the previous era takes on a glamour which was not present then. In this way Borodino becomes something directly alien to Tolstoy's conception, that of a particularly senseless piece of butchery; whilst the bungling of the Crimean campaign, with its horrifying rate of mortality from mismanagement and human callousness takes on a new aura.

Whatever the philosophical reflections caused by the pursuit of militaria in general, it may be said that the wargame in particular seems to provide many people with much satisfaction. One can be master of one's fate, and guide the destiny of nations. One can refight Waterloo and perhaps Napoleon will win (as the French have always maintained that he did). All the great battles and campaigns of history can be enacted on a table 12ft by 5ft, and, if one does not wish to follow the tactics or strategy that brought about historical victory and defeat, one can invent one's own battles, without having to weigh the imponderables that occur on an actual battlefield.

A change has come over the wargame in the last few years. In the beginning it was simple, usually conducted by two fellow-enthusiasts in the privacy of their own homes, and with their own rules. Afterwards, tea with the family, a handshake, and the question 'All right for next week, at my house?' – and that was the end of it. Now, however, there are societies all over the world, thousands of enthusiasts young and not so young, masses of rules drawn up to cover all periods of history, and mammoth games in public, played by whole teams of enthusiasts. I cannot be certain, but I feel that I saw somewhere that one further education board has included the wargame in its syllabus, and perhaps, who knows, it may one day become a subject for a university degree.

I was asked recently to talk on the model soldier to the war-gaming group at a local grammar school, which has a session every Saturday from 9 to 5.30 p.m. When asked his reasons for playing, one young boy said that he liked the tiny models so much that he wished to do something with them, as he was unsatisfied with just putting them 'on show'; which seems to me to be as good an answer as any.

The enthusiasm with which the game is played has been responsible for the upsurge of makers of tiny models expressly for this purpose. One supposes that the exercise could be conducted equally well with non-military symbols representing the components of the contending forces, and that battles could be fought on any flat surface of a given area free from any type of embellishment. It must be admitted, however, that there is a great deal of pleasure to be had in playing chess with a set of beautifully carved men, rather than a stereotyped Staunton pattern, and the same applies to the wargame. Much ingenuity, therefore, goes into the simulation of the actual terrain, with its hills and counter-slopes, its rivers and streams, its woods and hedges, its towns, villages, hamlets and farmhouses. Many and varied are the materials pressed into service; indeed, on a number of occasions the result could well form a permanent diorama.

Inevitably, there are two schools of thought regarding this. The first is all for austerity, with mere indications of primary requirements in the symbolic form of home-made blocks, strips of coloured paper, and sand. The second is imbued with the spirit of exactitude, and expresses itself by coloured earth, grass and gravel as supplied by the model-railway scenic makers, trees and hedges of plastic composition, walls, gates and farmyard equipment from Herald, farm buildings and private houses from a number of sources, and entrenchments and strips of muddy, shell-torn ground from Bellona. The setting-up of this diorama-form engagement table must last longer than the actual conflict which takes place upon it.

When the Germans turned out in millions their ugly 20, 30 and 40mm semi-solids, they were intended for the amusement of children, and nothing else. However, they were seized on for campaign purposes by such enthusiasts as Stevenson and Osbourne; but with the advent of Britains the larger size was used by Wells and his brother and also by Jerome for his activities. Groves and Benoy may have anticipated the modern wargame when, in the 1930s, they issued a series of 30mm solids of the Peninsular War (now obtainable only by chance) which slotted into a footstand. It is certain, conversely, that the makers of quality tiny models – Niblett, Eriksson, Greenwood & Ball, and Stadden (and Alymer, although inferior in quality) had no thought of the wargame when they produced them. They were merely exercising their preference for a delightful size (although Stadden soon went over to the wargame with other models). In a similar way, one feels that the 25–30mm works of art of Surén, Higgins, Hinchliffe and Minot are too lovely as individual pieces to be hidden in the anonymity of massed ranks. Nor, because of their size, do the small models of Starlux (although they are apparently designed for this purpose) or the 40mm of Elastolin and Berliner, seem appropriate. The German flats have their supporters, but one feels that the fragility of the models places too much onus on the player, when the careless sweep of an exultant or a frustrated arm may cause irrevocable damage.

One of the earliest makers catering exclusively for the wargamer was Jack Scruby, of the United States. He built up private armies of his own, later turning out masses of models which are still available from his workshop. Similar in content, but of far higher quality, was Bussler; also the Thomas models which are still being made, are exquisite, whilst Stadden, Gammage and Hinton form a triumvirate which covers practically every period, and they are still adding to their respective outputs.

Up to a few years ago the range of each maker was predictable: the Napoleonic wars, of course, the American Civil War, and the Crimean War. Owing, however, to the increasing interest displayed in wars of every period, the range has widened remarkably; probably the only period that is not well represented is the Middle Ages. The newly awakened fascination of the two World Wars, and the projection into the remote ages, encouraged and fostered by the Society of Ancients, has provided a new and interesting facet to the making of tiny figures, and a number of makers are doing their best to cope with the increasing demand for something entirely new.

Greenwood & Ball's Garrison range, designed by Braithwaite, is remarkable for its technique, its sense of period, and, quite important, the quality of its presentation. They were the first to cater for lovers of ancient times, and they set an example for other makers. Another firm, parallel in content and achievement, is that of Hinchliffe. Their 20 and 25mm models are the result of the joint efforts of Frank Hinchliffe and Peter Gilder, with Donovan Longley as master pattern maker. Turning out on the average five new models a week, they first announced their products for sale in October 1969, and since then they have proliferated. The models of the ancient world produced by these two firms have much in common. Craftsmanship is excellent, and the models are desirable for individual careful painting and display outside the wargame. Truly it can be said of both that they fulfil all the requirements, enabling the collector to people his wargame table not in imagination, but in reality, with the troops of the Greeks and Romans, and also of their auxiliaries, together with their barbarian antagonists and 'lesser tribes without the law'. The appearance of these models for painting, created the question of authentic colours, which gave rise to intensive and specialised research into a comparatively new and most rewarding field that is far from complete.

Both go further, and are equally strong in later periods of history, and Hinchliffe has a number of special 'personality' figures. Besides these, there are artillery pieces of beautiful workmanship: indeed, Hinchliffe himself commenced with these, and it was on them that his fame first rested. Their range was fully expressed by a 'Waterloo' comprising seven thousand models, first exhibited in Glasgow in April 1973.

Another firm to make 'ancients' is Miniature Figurines, whose owner, Neville Dickinson, was originally connected with Peter Gilder in a venture named Alberken. Upon Gilder's departure Dickinson redesigned what had already been made, and was soon joined by a number of other designers (including Neil Butcher, David and Richard Higgs, and David Hutchings) all as enthusiastic as himself. The most prolific of wargame figure-makers, the firm has a fantastic output which is constantly being added to; it features practically every known engagement, including such items as a Carthaginian war-elephant, a landau, and Samurai warriors. Readers of wargaming books and journals are likely to see more photographs of Miniature Figurines models than those of any other maker, past or present.

Their earlier horses were of a most haphazard size, varying from between 20 and even 40mm with complete impunity (horse and rider cast in one piece), but the scale is now more constant. Looking with an impartial eye at a cross-section, with all honesty it cannot be said that, even with careful painting, they more than just hold their own as individual pieces; but seen *en masse* they are certainly what the average wargamer requires: quantity, cheapness, sound workmanship, and variety. Of the latter there is abundance; quality has however, sometimes been sacrificed for price, and much tedious work is necessary in cleaning the flash off the castings.

The welter of scales that one encounters nowadays hardly seems necessary, and at times causes one to long for a latterday Britains or Heinrichsen. Dickinson, for example, makes his models in 5, 15, 20 and 25mm. Leicester Micromodels have medieval troops with portions of fortifications to match in 5mm, and R. B. and J. R. Styles (Heroics) cover World War II in all its aspects in 6mm. Peter Laing on the other hand makes a range of models in 15mm. These began with the period of 1700–30, and his intention is 'to cover, as completely as possible, the personnel and equipment of the period' and later additions of continental troops of the same era will be included. Laing specifically intends them for use in dioramas, but undoubtedly the wargamers will use them. In the meantime there is an ancient world group, a feudal range (Norman infantry and cavalry and mounted Saracens) and the American Revolution. The size of the model does not allow for any particular elegance, and they can scarcely be shown individually. Whatever reservations one may have about the necessity of such minute figures (and, after all, Siborne produced this size over a hundred years ago) one imagines that the enthusiast will find a use for them, and at the price experiments that prove abortive can hardly affect the pocket.

Returning to slightly larger scales, the 20mm models of E. Alexandre (Jacklex) are quite outstanding in their quality, and the presentation is remarkably good. The range covers the colonial period (1890–1900), the Regular Indian Army, the Zulu War, the Northwest Frontier, and the American Civil War. One outstanding example is the mounted Indian army trooper. The models repay careful painting. Modern troops in the same scale by Almark, and designed by Stadden, are also of very good quality.

William Lamming features the contestants at Waterloo, both mounted and on foot, together with artillery. His 25mm medieval knights are very welcome. The horses are made in two pieces, which interlock accurately, the helms are detachable, and there is a choice of crests. Artillery pieces and siege weapons complete the collection. The Napoleonic period is also made by A. Graham (Silvercross), together with the British of World War I, and an interesting early British chariot. J. D. Johnston (Douglas Miniatures) having commenced by making 54mm models, has also turned his hand to those of half the size. In addition he is recasting the old World War I figures originally issued by Holloday (Skybird). Harry Norey's

Page 69 (*above*) Medieval (foot): 54 and 56mm figures of colourful character. On raised stands: Mokarex; Imrie-Risley (Burgundian gunner with bombard); Hinton (adapted); Douglas; Imrie-Risley; Valiant (El Cid). On ground: Hinton (Henry V); Gammage (adapted); Stadden; Valiant; Stadden; Monarch; Frontier (King John); Frontier; Lasset (2); (*below*) An unusual and attractive approach, depicting a group of officers before dinner. Models and furniture by Major Robert Rowe (Ensign Miniatures).

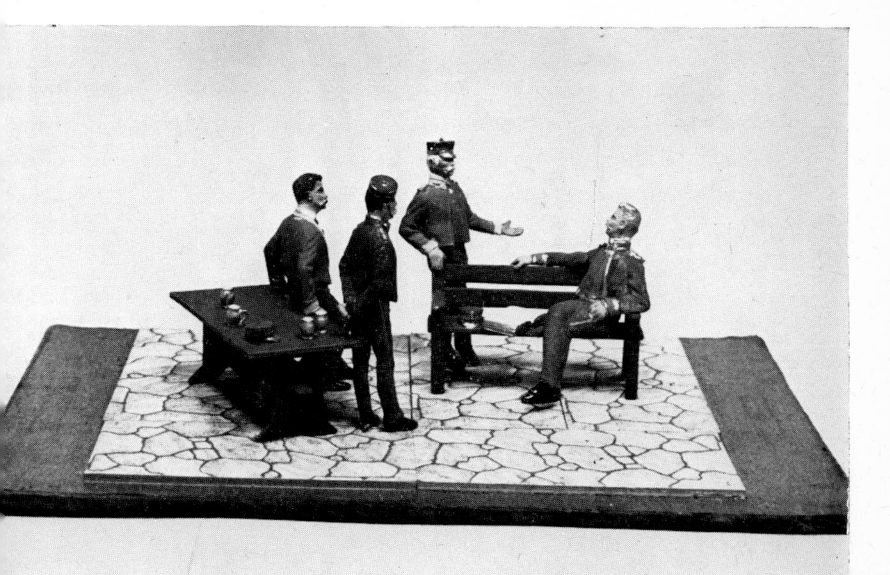

Page 70 (*above*) A selection of American models, all but one in 54–56mm by prominent US makers. On raised stands: Roman legionary (Old Guard); Rochambeau and Washington (both by Vallance). On ground: Infantry, Legion of the USA, 1795 (Greer, painted by him); Rogers' Rangers (Vallance); Russian infantryman, 1812 (Old Guard, painted by Le Gloahec); World War II fighter pilot (Imrie-Risley, 90mm); Czar Nicholas II (Old Guard); Hessian, 1775 (Lance, painted by Cooke); Andrew Jackson (Valiant); Von Steuben (Greer, painted by him); (*below*) A further selection of 54–56mm models by leading American makers. On raised stands: Napoleon in Egypt (Valiant); US Army Special Force, 1960 (Aristo-Merité); 1st Sergeant of Panzers, Afrika Korps (Cavalier); German shock trooper, 1943 (Valiant); Texas ranger (The Scrimshander); Third Louisiana Infantry, 1862 (TBS). On ground: Death's Head Hussar, 1808–15 (Squadron/Rubin); Timucua, Florida Indian chief 1565 (TBS); Swedish Guard grenadier, Leipzig, 1813 (Valiant); grenadier, 1st Regiment Imperial Guard, 1812 (Stewart); cavalry trooper at Wounded Knee, 1890 (Squadron/Rubin); Legion of the USA, 1794 (Stewart); naval officer (van Tubergen); Jim Bridger, Indian scout (The Scrimshander); Confederate major (Cavalier); Mexican zapatta (Squadron/Rubin).

Warrior Miniatures (originally 30mm, now 25) although not in the first rank, do help to fill out the ancient world, the Normans, the Civil War and the Napoleonic wars. Quite outstanding in the latter period are the models of Barry Minot. Few of these have appeared at the time of writing, but already it is evident that they will have an outstanding success. He is doing what the early makers of flats sometimes did, that is, joining two or more figures on one base, as in the following examples: a wounded British infantryman assisted by a colleague, three Frenchmen around a standard, and a wounded recumbent soldier attended by a cantonière.

Whilst still carefully and frugally nursing a small residue of the original 'Jason' Marlburians and Civil War models of Higgins, Phoenix is producing 20 and 30mm bands of the British line regiments, the Guards Brigade, and Highland and Lowland regiments, together with the Napoleonic period, the Sudan Expedition, and Greeks (no lances or pikes supplied), as well as one or two field pieces and armoured vehicles under the name 'Renown'.

In America Scruby's models are still available, and those of Bussler on occasion, but undoubtedly the finest are the 20mm figures originally made by Thomas and still purchaseable. These are beautiful little models, the weapons more delicately formed than usual. A word regarding these small scale weapons in general will, perhaps, be appropriate. Owing to the difficulties inherent in casting tiny objects, any projecting part will normally be exaggerated. This is particularly evident in cast spears, such as those of the Greeks, and in the lances of the Middle Ages, whilst swords are particularly susceptible to an over-emphasis which can make a rapier look like a cutlas. It is quite common, therefore, to find a landschnecht wielding a pike of such thickness that he would be unable to pick it up, let alone use it. The weapons are so frail that sandpapering is difficult, and the makers of the better-quality models endeavour to supply these adjuncts to the correct scale. In some cases, however, it may be necessary to file off the weapon completely, drill a hole in the receiving hand, and insert a piece of copper wire of a more appropriate thickness.

The biggest impact on wargaming circles was probably made by the introduction in the 1960s of the Airfix 20mm flexible plastic model. Britains had made a tentative but short lived start with this medium, but Airfix really cornered the market. Their forty-eight man packs, the figures attached to the sprues or draining channels, and issued at a ridiculously cheap price, put the collecting of tiny models within the reach of everyone. It was possible to build up a complete army in the easiest and cheapest possible manner. For example, the somewhat clumsy Robin Hood bowmen could be made into a rabble of peasants, and the Sheriff of Nottingham regulars augmented by the purchase of a given number of boxes. Although on the whole well designed, the inherent disadvantages of alkathene have not yet been overcome, so that lances wave at curiously shaped angles, the tiny pegs on the underside of the horses' hooves are stubbornly reluctant to slot into the holes in the somewhat thick bases, a large amount of flash has to be removed, paint is readily rubbed off, and they are easily knocked over.

Before their advent certain periods had not been fully covered by the existing makers of metal models, and the enthusiast set about converting his Airfix models into something entirely different. This was not just a case of altering the posture of a figure by alternate hot and cold water, the lopping off of a piece of equipment, or the making of a different weapon, but the reconstitution of a complete unit from, say, the American Civil War to the Trooping of the Colour. Much ingenuity was displayed, including the pinning of limbs and the making of uniforms from tissuepaper. Much of this effort has now been eliminated with the introduction, by Garrison and Hinchliffe and Miniature Figurines, of all-embracing armies, and one imagines that Airfix models will now be used without further butchery.

An attempt has recently been made by A. C. Collett (Springwood Models) with polystyrene models in 25mm scale. They are issued as a pack of forty-eight, each attached to the sprue, and divided into four equal groups of British, French, Prussians and Russians of 1815. A coloured guide to the uniforms and standards is issued with each packet. Only one stance is represented, that of a marching infantryman. Better known, and emanating from a firm of much longer standing, are Segom's 25mm foot and mounted Napoleonic and British models. These, besides being well designed, have the advantage of a number of 'combination' figures, a device well known to collectors of flats. The standards, however, are on the small size, and one cannot really visualise the models' suitability for the wargame.

It is self-evident that, with a number of makers issuing similar ranges, combinations of models of the same era in the same scale either for wargaming or for a diorama, can be readily affected. Thus, Miniature Figurines' foot and Hinchliffe's cavalry and artillery blend perfectly together, as do Garrison's and Hinchliffe's 'ancients', whilst the medieval troops of Airfix, Miniature Figurines, Garrison and Lamming could all be combined into one larger army.

In startling contrast to the tiny models are the large ones. The products turned out in 54mm scale form the basis of collecting all over the world, but it would be wise to point out that there are many variations from 52 to 56 or even 60mm, few makers keeping strictly to the ideal as evolved by William Britain. Of the older makers, Courtenay, Gammage, and Greenwood were scrupulous in this regard, and so was Stadden in his early days. Imrie is always more or less near the target, as are Frontier and Jackboot, and whilst Lasset and Jac tend more towards 56mm, and Hinton at times to 60mm, Ping has always been a little under the standard size. It must be remembered that this height is reckoned from the sole of the foot to the crown of the head of a standing figure, irrespective of headgear. It might appear at first sight to be a quibble, but these differences are magnified when for example a Courtenay horse is placed near a much larger version by Kirk or Trophy. On one occasion Brunoe sent me a delightful female model. I commissioned a male companion from another maker, only to find on its arrival that the latter was fractionally smaller, thus spoiling the whole effect. The discrepancies may sometimes be overcome by placing a group of models in diorama form, and slightly building up the ground under the shorter figure, thus creating the illusion of height. It is less easy where horsemen are concerned.

Until quite recent years two or three artists made models static in nature for presentation or decorative purposes, and then mainly in the form of plaster composition. This is a medium that has a long history, as evinced by the set of models of Franz Josef and his staff, one set owned by the late Baron Huber, another by the late Marcel Baldet, and a third by Maître Phillipot. Huber had a number of other equestrian models of this type, such as one depicting General Williams recently on sale at 'Tradition'. Coppin and Synge-Hutchinson produced a number of equestrians for the National Army Museum and naval types for the National Maritime Museum, whilst Morrison's figures in barbola and Cawood's in carved wood are well known. The supreme examples are the series of carved wood polychrome statuettes supervised by Pilkington Jackson for the Scottish National Museum, and the long series in wood, plaster and natural materials made by Helmut Krauhs for various museums in Austria. Jackson has since experimented in all types of material, including aluminium, synthetic resin, fibreglass and laminated metals. However, as these models are mainly over three feet in height, they can be regarded as outside the mainstream. Less large in size are the models of Lelièpvre, Rousselot, Pranzetti and Chiappa. These together with the plaster models of Willetts and Patmore (now both retired), the fibreglass figures by Turner, the woodcarvings by Rendall, the original Sentry Box, and those produced by Don and Honey Ray, Arthur (father and son), and Arquette, are all obviously meant for a museum or a special occasion. In 1971 their ranks were joined by Ronald Cameron, with a splendid range of models in 120mm in metal (a trooper, hussars, grenadier à cheval de la garde, garde lanciers, garde grenadiers, Empress dragoons (all 1812), together with Nansouty and d'Hautpoul, both Generals of Cuirassiers, Jérome Bonaparte, and Colonel-General of Carabiniers). These have been exceeded in size by Preiser of Nuremberg, with 250mm eighteenth-century troops and a set of four Napoleonic types in 300mm, imported by Warneford from Italy, the name of whose designer cannot be disclosed by the importer. Both these two last sets are in hard plastic.

Between these outsize models and the normal satisfying 54mm range are the now-famous Stadden 90mm figures – beautifully designed, skillfully produced, in good postures, and admirable when painted. So far, subjects are fairly equally divided between British and French troops of 1810–15, with the additional figures of Wellington and Napoleon, two infantrymen on manoeuvres, one, a dragoon, wearing a plumed helmet and with a carbine (1895), the other an infantry private in Slade-Wallace equipment with a Lee-Metford, together with a trooper of the Household Cavalry and guardsman of the Coldstream Guards (both of 1970).

In the same size are the models of Maurene Sandoe (Men o'War) which were first offered for sale in February 1973. They are available either assembled or in kit form, and include a French Dutch lancer (1812–14), a British trumpeter and NCO in campaign dress (1810–15), and a Jacobean musketeer. The faces are full of expression, and the sculpting crisp. Miss Sandoe (Mrs M. J. Lane) entered the military model world via various colleges, culminating in the stained glass department of the Royal College of Art. Thence she went to the studio of Russell Gammage, and pays tribute to the thorough training she received.

In the United States, also, the larger model has its adherents. Lionel Forrest, known for some years as a gifted 'amateur' and painter, set up his own firm of Superior Models, which issues an impressive collection of troops of the American Revolution, including portraits of Washington, Burgoyne and Kosciuszko, two mounted knights in combat, a mounted Cortes, a Charlemagne on a rearing horse, an officer of the Bengal Lancers, a Renaissance field, a 7.5mm German World War II Howitzer, an 88mm anti-aircraft gun, and a German 5cm anti-tank gun, all with the requisite crews. The models are beautifully sculpted, and remarkably free from flash or mould-joins. Another range is made by Ron Hinote (Little Generals) which, whilst not reaching quite the same standard of Superior Models, are still interesting. So far the releases include a British pikeman of 1660, a Dervish warrior, a German infantryman World War II, a machine-gunner warming his hands at a fire, a Highlander of 1880, a French foreign legionaire, three models from World War I, a Prussian grenadier, and Hindenburg. Hinote appears to have had some initial difficulties with pitting on his original models, but has now rectified this by the use of a better quality rubber for the moulds, and by casting in tin alloy rather than in lead.

In December 1970 I received through the post a small group of exceptionally well painted models of a size I had not previously encountered, and which I had some difficulty in establishing. The accompanying letter explained that these were the first products of a new firm calling themselves Series 77, and that they were the results of an amalgamation between John Tassell and Pat Bird. Perhaps on further examination the legs of the models were a little stout, and the faces subject to the usual trade over-painting, but the quality was obvious, and I immediately despatched an enthusiastic letter of appreciation to the makers, following this with an equally enthusiastic notice to my society journal. Since those days the partnership has dissolved, and Pat Bird has remade the original models in a tin alloy and in a true 77mm size. From their inception these models have become amazingly popular, and, although not qualifying for the designation of statuette, they surprisingly enough do not appear out of scale when placed with normal size figures. The usual British and French of the Waterloo period predominate, but there is also a set of British World War II pilots, a group of mounted and foot landschnechts (one with an undersize detachable sallet), troops of the English Civil War, and a remarkable set of Greeks, together with a noble chariot. If one were to be hypercritical, one would perhaps take exception to the somewhat vacuous expression on the face of the nude Greek warrior and on that of Apollo, but one example in particular, that of a military man carrying his small son, is particularly pleasing. The various issues as they came out were distinguished as Series 1, Series 2, Series 3, and so on, but as soon as the original models were remade, they were replaced by a new series, which made listing difficult. Taken as a whole, this is a group of figures worthy of the most careful and sensitive painting.

As far back as 1955 Georges Fouillé began making models in 150mm size. Beautifully designed and cast, and elegantly painted, with belts, cartridge boxes etc, added separately, they are among the finest of model soldiers, both in their conception and in their grace and elegance. The majority are of the Napoleonic period (some mounted) but there is also a Lauzun Legion trooper during the American Revolution. They are obtainable from The Soldier Shop, at prices ranging from $100 (£43) to $250 (£108). Christian Fabre, also, was early in this field of the large-sized figure, and has made a fair number of these, ranging from a German World War II officer to a Napoleonic hussar, and including a World War II German standard bearer and a poilu of the earlier war. They are hand cast to order.

The lastest size to make its appearance is the 75mm. Raymond Lamb, long known as a splendid painter of models, came to an agreement with Hinchliffe Models and Armour Accessories (the main Historex agent in England) whereby he would design models, Hinchliffe would cast them, and Armour Accessories would market them. The first five models, issued in kit form in September 1973, are all of French troops of 1805–7 and are remarkable for the individual characterisations. Imrie has also produced some models in this size, several of the

American Revolution and a pair of World War II pilots, one German, the other English. In this instance, however, the models are moulded in one piece, and consequently need only to be painted.

The very latest model in this size of which we have heard is again designed by Ray Lamb, and produced by Hinchliffe, in September 1973. It is an incredible *saburai*, consisting of twenty-six pieces of the most exquisite craftsmanship, each a miracle of technique and artistry. There is tremendous scope here for painting a breath-taking model, and the size in which it is made allows for the correct positioning of the pieces, which in a smaller model might well-nigh prove impossible. The finished model is to be classed as among the most remarkable ever to be made.

7

FLATS

Up to the middle of the 1960s it was possible to visit the museum of the Royal United Service Institution in the basement of the Banqueting Hall in Whitehall, in order to view the outstanding collection of dioramas using the traditional continental flats. They were conceived by Otto Gottstein and executed by a team led by Denny C. Stokes, assisted by such enthusiasts as W. Y. Carman and P. Clendennin. Gottstein's object was to display a selection of the great events in English history in appreciation of the welcome that he, as a proscribed Jew, had experienced in England after his flight from Hitlerian Germany. Beginning with the landing of the Romans, the dioramas depicted such famous engagements as Hastings, Plassey, Crecy, Marston Moor and Balaclava, and the results were achieved by the use of thousands of specially selected flats drawn from the stocks of the best continental makers, and painted by teams of experts. The final diorama was the first to use 20mm solids by Greenwood & Ball.

It was the first time that many collectors could see and appreciate the tremendous variety of modern German flats, but, unfortunately, the subsequent dispersal of the cases to various museums has deprived later generations of an opportunity of seeing these marvellous little figures in large quantities, and to many these are still almost completely unknown. This is a great pity, as model-soldier collecting virtually began with them, and they are still the main type of figure collected on the Continent. We have become so used to seeing dioramas composed of 20 and 30mm and even 54mm models that the possibilities displayed by flats has been temporarily forgotten. Few dealers will import them, as trading procedures are difficult, and few collectors except the most ardent can afford to battle with the customs duties and VAT levied by the authorities.

The one attempt (made by Carman and Gottstein) to manufacture an English product met with failure. It has been left to a few sensitive individuals in England to keep their memory green. As a nation we have taken little interest in them just as in Germany they have rejected their own Heydes and Haffners. But flats have in their own way much to offer. If one assumes that the purpose of collecting military miniatures is to relive the past then they enable this to be done in profusion. If one seeks historical accuracy, it is here. If one is governed by size, flats are far more economical on space than solids. If cost is a consideration, they are no more expensive than wargame figures. If one wishes to construct a tableau or a diorama, they are far more adaptable than their larger counterparts. If one looks for beauty of craftsmanship, it is here in abundance, and the pleasure of painting them is just as great.

As with hollow-casts, critical assessment of the standard flats of Heinrichsen and Allgeyer and the like came in the early part of the present century, and serious students of history and art banded together to encourage the making of models of a more acceptable quality. Immense historical research was undertaken, and gradually a new school of designers and engravers emerged, together with 'editors' (agents) prepared to distribute the resultant models. These were at first confined primarily to the collectors' groups composed of enthusiasts who eagerly purchased them to replace the inadequate commercial productions. The scale of 30mm was generally adopted, as giving greater scope for the engraving of detail, the metal was hardened, and experts undertook the painting. They were immensely varied in their scope, ranging over all periods of history, and each set consisted of a number of separate postures.

The necessity of making a separate mould for each of these models was later eliminated to a certain degree by the invention of the 'combination' figure, whereby a model consisted of several arms, heads, legs and weapons in different positions, so that extraneous ones could be cut away.

The emphasis was no longer on masses of figures sold by weight, in which detail and engraving was of secondary consideration. Now each model underwent a thorough scrutiny before it was issued, and the object was no longer the making of colossal dioramas where refinements were not necessary. Dioramas there certainly were, and one of the prime functions of the flat is its use in this context. At the same time, it was realised that a flat could be used in a diorama and yet still be a beautiful if tiny object in its own right, and anyone fortunate enough to have seen the Royal United Service Institution dioramas would have appreciated how engraving, painting and action were blended together in the most satisfying settings.

However, it is not necessary to create a vast picture to get the best out of flats. True, there are a number of sets available which include a great number of separate models, many capable of modification, thus creating more, such as Scholtz's 'Choral of Leuthen', and his 'Retreat from Moscow' (divided into three sections: the 'Retreat', the 'Crossing of the Beresina', and the 'Burning of the Standards'), Müller's 'Tannenberg', and Ochel's 'Coronation of Charles V'. Heinrichsen indeed also created vast sets, but many of the models were mere repetition, whereas the modern figures cover every detail of the particular event illustrated. Small groups are highly acceptable, as Denny Stokes showed on numerous occasions, half a dozen well painted and arranged figures creating a satisfying group; many of the sets cater for separate sections within the main battle, as in Gottstein-Blum's 'Battle of Morat'. There are some collectors who abjure dioramas, and are perfectly content to collect flats for their beauty, to lovingly paint them and display them in boxes or in cabinets.

One great advantage of the flat over the solid is that works by different makers can be easily displayed together in one setting. For one thing, the scale is far more constant than that of the solid, and the general level of skilful production is extremely high. Therefore one can successfully build up a large army by incorporating the works of several makers without any ambiguities or irrelevant figures or sizes appearing, as one can, to a certain extent, with wargame figures.

The germ of a superior model was first introduced by Hilpert in the eighteenth century in his special, probably commissioned, series, and continued by various makers as a sideline to their mass-production. Some of the best models came from Strasbourg, and in Hanover those of J. E. du Bois are well worthy of consideration. (A set of his Romans fetched a good price at auction a few years ago.) Rieche, also, produced a range of portrait models, designed by Knotel, whilst such makers as Meyerheine and Schweitzer made charming civilian types.

The harvest planted by these early makers was reaped by such ardent collectors as Biebel, Gottstein and Müller. Primarily collectors, they turned with energy to the process of supplying their fellow enthusiasts. Such engravers as Sixtus Maier, Ludwig Frank, Hinsch, and Möhr began their delicate work, and Aloys Ochel, Gerhard Müller and F. C. Neckel carried out the marketing. The models could be purchased either as castings or factory painted. This type of painting is crude, and does little more than cover the model with an approximation to accuracy; it is better to purchase the castings, where the beauty of the engraving can be examined in detail. However, if one required a special job to be done (as in the case of the Whitehall dioramas) teams of expert painters were ready to devote their skill to these tiny figures. And what skill they possessed! When one considers that a very large number of models in dioramas such as these would of necessity be relegated to the background, it is incredible that such painting should be considered necessary. A professionally painted flat has to be seen to be believed, and an appropriate price is charged.

Today the number of designers, engravers and distributors engaged in the industry is truly remarkable, ranging from the large firms to those who occasionally make a model or add one to an existing range. The following can only be regarded as an indication of the full total of those engaged in the industry of flats, and the list of nearly every maker can be added to indefinitely:

Beck: (20mm) Prussians, 1760, 1920. *Blum:* Mamelukes; medievals. *Bolling:* 1870; 1914. *Braune:* Napoleonic. *Cortum:* Ancient world. *Droste:* Thirty Years' War. *Fohler:* Siege of Vienna; Thirty Years' War; Napoleonic; Boer War. *Franke:* Napoleonic. *Frauendorf:* Napoleonic; 1870; 1914. *Fritz:* Thirty Years' War; 1700; Turks. *Gottstein:* Ancient world; English kings and queens; Normans; 1400–1600; Charles the Bold; the Valois (with *Carman, Blum*). *Hafer:* Seven Years' War; Napoleonic; Bavaria 1805–15, 1864–70; Classical; Biblical; Ancient world. *Herbu:* Frederick the Great. *Hodapp:* Napoleonic. *Kebbel:* 1525 Peasant's War; Seven Years' War; 1790; Napoleonic; World Wars I and II artillery. *Lecke:* (mainly an engraver) 1756. *Loy:* American Revolutionary War. *Mauke:* Napoleonic. *Müller:* Crusaders, Saracens; Middle Ages; 1500–1600; Hindenburg. *Nahde:* Napoleonic. *Neckel:* Ancient world; medieval; Landschnechts; Franco-Prussian war; American Revolution; American Civil War; Wild West; Americans and Japanese, 1900–18; World War I; Third Reich; Indian Mutiny; South-West Africa; Napoleonic; Burgundians; field guns. *Ochel* (Kilia): Ancient world; Dark Ages; medieval; Aztecs and Conquistadores; Landschnechts; Thirty Years' War; war-elephants; siege weapons. *Retter:* Ancient world; medieval; World Wars I and II. *Romund:* Prehistory; Seven Years' War; French Foreign Legion; Wild West. *Rucker:* World War II. *Sandow:* South-West Africa. *Scharlowsky:* Germany 1913. *Scheibert:* Napoleonic. *Schmidt:* Napoleonic. *Scholtz* (Berlin Zinnfiguren): Hannibal and Scipio; medieval; Landschnechts; Seven Years' War; Frederick the Great; Retreat from Moscow; also very large flats. *Sima*

(Sixtus Maier): Napoleonic; Swiss 1830–8; Franco-Prussian War. *Sollner:* (20mm) Thirty Years' War; Napoleonic; Franco-Prussian War; World War II. *Staar:* Louis XIV. *Tobinnus:* Romans; medieval; Landschnechts (Pavia); Thirty Years' War; Franco-Prussian War; Boer War; German East Africa (some 20mm). *Trips:* Ancient world; Napoleonic. *Wagner:* Seven Years' War. *Waibel:* Napoleonic. *Wollrath:* Medieval kings and queens.

From the very beginning of the industry the makers were not confined to military subjects; the eighteenth century provided many delightful pleasure gardens, zoological scenes and groups of civilian activities. Carriages were particularly popular, and, when the early railways began tin-figure manufacturers were quickly off the mark. Ships, also, and natural objects such as trees and shrubs were made in great numbers, and even farmhouses and complete villages in the flat. Today they are eagerly sought for on account of the rococo or early Victorian charm. It is good to see that later engravers have commemorated many an activity of interest to ordinary people – butter-markets and fêtes of all descriptions, country and town fairs, hawking parties, medieval weddings, the chase, opera, and drama. Hafer, for example, has created a whole series of historic scenes from biblical history, including fowling on the Nile (from actual wall-paintings), Salome, a slave market, Adam and Eve, David and Goliath, Samson and Delilah, Moses in the bulrushes, the worship of the Golden Calf, and Judith and Holofernes. From classical times come the Rape of Europa, Phryne and Praxiteles, Nefertiti (sculpted by Thutmos), Leda and the swan, the Amazons, and bull-jumping in ancient Crete. A number of these sets have the necessary furniture and other accessories, so that little tableaux may be made. Beck has constructed a series of characters from the Siegfried saga, and Braune a Leonardo de Vinci with the model for his 'Mona Lisa'. Scholtz has a delightful group showing a street photographer in the early twentieth century, and his extensive rococo garden is a sheer delight; whilst two of

Winkelmüller's (Wimor) sets are particularly attractive: an 'Arabian Nights', and a medieval Burgundian wedding. Perhaps the most beautiful of all is a stag-hunting party of the early eighteenth century, which includes equestrians and equestriennes, a picnic party, a tree full of wild fowl, a pavilion, and a monarch entering his carriage.

Other diverse civilian subjects worthy of mention are Goya with his models (Braune); Riemenshneider woodcarving an altar-piece (Braune again); Burgundian farmers and peasants with children, sheep and pigs (Albrecht); a peasant dance of 1630 (Grunewald); Hansa port civilians (Neumeister); Minnesingers (Grunewald); wine makers (Mentz); a dentist at work in the seventeenth century (Braune); Pope Julius II with the 'Apollo Belvedere' (Sima); an eighteenth-century German hunt (Wimor); the Witches' Kitchen from 'Faust' (Unger). These are, of course, only a fraction of the figures available, but even this very brief résumé will be sufficient to show how far advanced the production of civilians in flats is as compared with solids. Indeed, the whole *raison d'être* of the flat is a representation of the inhabitants of the world and their activities in all times, the fact that military distractions form a large part of these activities is merely incidental.

It is this factor that raises the flat above the solid in its philosophy. To a certain extent the choice was forced on the Germans after World War II, as they were forbidden to make military 'toys', which is why one sees little of the present interest which is displayed by the English-speaking collectors of World War II and all its incredible assembly of armoured vehicles and the like. In fact, the latest book on flats, emanating from Eastern Germany (E. Ortmann, *Zinnfiguren Einst und Jetzt*, Leipzig, 1972), devotes only a very small portion of its text to models other than flats, and illustrates merely three models by Eriksson and an atrociously badly painted group of Staddens.

Flats did not remain the prerogative of Germany and Strasbourg for long, and there is evidence of their manufacture in Sweden as early as 1760, in Italy about ten years later, and even in remote Finland in 1780. In Portugal they were made by at least one engraver, Simon Roullé, and Spain followed suit about 1830. In Denmark a few moulds dating from around 1800 have been found but not identified, but one maker at least, Høy, signed his name on a large equestrian flat of Frederick VII (c1850). From about 1840 Sanchez in Spain and Santessonska Tenngjuteriet and Tenngjuteriet Mars produced a large number; some of the latter are still obtainable. One of the most recent Swedish designers was Georg Rössner (died 1973) who reverted to the larger sizes of the eighteenth century for his admirable sets of civilians and Persian fairy tales. Another fine Swedish editor is Thorold Sivhed, who concentrates on the Seven Years' War, sometimes incorporating several figures on one stand. The designs are made by Martin Block, Roland Backman and Willie Ericson, and engraved by Lecke, Frank or M. Knoll. There are no native makers of flats in Holland, but on occasions the collecting society has figures from Dutch history engraved for them.

Shortly before World War II, a group of enthusiasts, artists, historians and engravers, got together in France and began to produce beautiful sets of flats. Designed by Rousselot, Hamel, Armont, Bombled and Martin, engraved by Maier, Hahnemann and Frank, painted by Rousselot and Madame Métayer, they were placed on the market by Mignot and immediately attracted the attention of sensitive students of history. They are still available, and may be seen at the Mignot headquarters, 1 Rue de Vieux Colombier, near St Sulpice, in Paris, where they may be chosen by consulting the catalogue. The most outstanding, as might be expected, is the very large set of Napoleonic troops, especially the Emperor at the Pyramids, and a number of subjects depict several figures on one stand. Less distinguished, surprisingly, is the Joan of Arc set, the figures are all in a static position, comparing unfavourably with those made by Ochel. Other, finer, models, are chariots of ancient times, Nubian war-elephants, the Field of the Cloth of Gold,

Page 87 (*above*) The French model at its best. A collection of 54mm solids by Roger Berdou, the supreme maker of models of this kind; (*below*) Swedish mastery: General von Döbeln, 1808, a hero of the war against Russia. A fine 54mm solid lead model by Magnus Schreiber.

Page 88 (*above*) Scandinavian elegance: Swedish and Danish makers are meticulous in the finish of their models. The two figures on raised stands are a Russian cavalryman, 1918, by Eriksson and a Swedish Grenadier, Seven Years War, by Brunoe. The central Roman scene, made by Brunoe, is flanked on the left by a Swedish hussar c1850 by Eriksson, and on the right by Brunoe's Von Steuben. In front: marine gunner, Denmark 1800–14 by Høyer, Piper Findlater at Dargai, 1898, French officer with dog c1760 and a Swedish grenadier, Marlborough War, all by Brunoe; and a Swedish pikeman c1610–20 by Høyer (Isopon and balsa wood). All these models were painted by the maker; (*below*) Spain and Italy: on raised stands: 1st Regiment of Hussars, Rep Cisalpine, 1800 (Bormioli); British Guards Sergeant-Major, Pranzetti (carved wood); Marshal Berthier (Labayen); Dragon de la Garde; 7th Regiment of Cuirassiers (both by Almirall). On ground: officer, Carabinieri Piedmontese, 1833 (Bormioli); piper, 42nd Highlanders, 1815 (Almirall); Scottish clansman (Alcocer); fusilier, Chasseur de la Garde, 1814 (45mm, Alcocer); Spanish Civil War Infantry; Voluntario, 1st Battalion de Gerona, Carlist War, 1872–77 (both by Manuel). All the models were painted by the makers.

Cortes and the Aztecs, the Thirty Years' War (with Wallenstein's mule-chair) and the Franco-Prussian War.

Less embracing in their scope was a range of hussars by Boverat, designed and engraved by Pepin, who also produced several sets issued by Commandant Borie. Some of the finest designs are those issued by Ch F. Keller, one section devoted to the troops of Louis XV, another of Louis XVI, then The Hundred Swiss, next the Second Empire, and finally the Swiss Army (1912–35). These were issued in collaboration with Jean Brutsch. Two other series, one of French infrantry (1786), the other, representatives of the Cantons at the Occupation of Basle, conclude the military series. Brétignier has a large range of Napoleonic troops, and also of French army types of World War I, including artillery. As with Sivhed, the moulds are engraved in Germany by such masters as Lecke and Maier.

One of the difficulties inherent in the recording of flats is that one cannot give credit to one person when discussing a particular model. One can say a 'Courtenay' or a 'Gammage' and one knows what is meant; one cannot, however, say that a flat is a 'Frank' or a 'Lecke', as they are classified as engravers, and work for many editors. It is therefore usual to list them under the actual producer, such as Ochel, Neckel and the like. However, one normally finds the initials of both the editor and the engraver on the upper side of the footstand. One of the main reasons for the lack of interest in individuals and model-shops when acquiring flats is the difficulty of importing them from the Continent. At present one first has to find out the address of the individual editor, and then ask for the required figures to be sent. If he is not fully versed in the procedure, the recipient will find himself with a package bearing a declaration of value. Upon this will be clapped a swingeing import duty and VAT, in many cases almost equalling the original cost. But if the vendor posts the flats in small numbers of not more than a dozen in an ordinary long envelope, in practice the authorities do not seem to regard them as being subject to tax.

Unfortunately many editors are very bad business-men, and

either cannot read English or are unwilling to satisfy a collector. As far as trying to get any satisfaction from the eastern zone of Germany this is impossible. The only alternative in both cases is to try and find a reliable agent who handles the products of several editors. Such a one is Rudolf Donath, who has a high reputation for probity and ability. Of the private individuals I have always found Werner Scholtz and Walter Hafer most eager to oblige. In this country the two greatest collectors and the most willing to share their profound knowledge with other collectors are the Bantocks, father and son, to whose regular notes on flats as published in collecting journals, tribute is here paid.

8

THE PLASTIC REVOLUTION

Historians may well call the latter half of the present century the 'Age of Plastic', and certainly there is hardly an area in which it has not taken control. It has shown itself increasingly in the manufacture of toys, with results at once beneficial and disastrous, as many a parent soon discovers as he ruefully surveys the newly purchased but soon broken polythene doll's pram or mechanical digger. So far as toy soldiers are concerned the results have been mixed. Cheapness of production in mass has meant a flood of models that have not stood up to everyday use, and there has been a tendency by many manufacturers to sacrifice design to mass production. The very nature of their chemical composition has hardened the heart of many a collector, and they are in certain circles consigned to outer darkness as not worthy of consideration. Certainly they will not have the lasting strength of even hollow-cast metal, and what can be done with paint that flakes off after a little handling? A mass of maltreated plastic models is a much more revolting sight than a group of battered Britains.

The obvious advantage is price and quantity. Less obvious is the much greater range of action available and the possibilities of better detail and reproduction than are feasible in hollow-cast. One has only to compare the face of a Britains' hollow-cast with that of a plastic 'Eyes Right' to notice the startling advance by the latter; such is the nature of plastic that every tiny portion of the mould is automatically reproduced when the molten material sets; the onus for a good model is therefore on the designer.

Having seen hollow-casts under production, it was instructive to watch the process of the making of a plastic model, this time not at Britains' headquarters, but at their King's Cross Road plant. There I saw the original plasticine model made by Roy Selwyn-Smith, the moulds that had been made from it, and the way in which the model is produced. The plastic arrives in different colours, and an appropriate one is chosen. Thus, if the predominant colour is to be red, a red plastic is used, if blue, a blue one, and so on. This eliminates a large amount of subsequent painting. Britains call the plastic components 'alkathene', and this is the type normally found in this country and in many others. It arrives in the form of tiny granules, and when liquified at immense heat are released in a stream to pour into the moulds, arranged in a wheel-like formation; the channels down which the liquid pours, being as it were the spokes, become the stems or 'sprues' from which the resultant model or portion of the model is subsequently removed.

Alkathene is a fairly strong substance not unlike highly compressed rubber. In 54mm scale it is sufficiently rigid to cause little distortion in lances or rifles, but in smaller sizes its strength diminishes, and distortion occurs. It can also be used to produce fine objects such as the thongs of a whip (as in Britain's 'Polar Exploration' set) or the bridle of a horse. Many other firms make their models of a similar composition. Up to quite recent times the Germans made their models of a mixture of sawdust, resin and glue, but the latest type is quite different, having a more metallic feel, especially when it is flicked with the finger. The better French and Spanish models are of the alkathene type, but many of those made in the United States, Italy and the countries of the European Eastern bloc are somewhat softer and flexible, and improbable and impossible results are obtainable, particularly in larger sizes, in the cheaper stores, especially in Czechoslovakia.

The best British alkathene models are without a doubt those by Britains-Herald. Originally created by Roy Selwyn-Smith for a firm called Zang, Britains soon realised their potential, and their greater marketing facilities ensured that they would have a world-wide market. Whilst following the firm's tradition of the regiments and the bands of the British Army (the 'Eyes Right' series), models of many other types are available, including the modern army with missile-firing mortars, the medieval times (with siege weapons), the American War of Independence (with cannon) and the Civil War (complete with a mounted gun-team), the English Civil War, the Canadian Northwest Mounted Police, a British naval cannon and crew of 1800. The riders are removable.

Their 'Swoppet' range was designed to meet the needs of purchasers wishing to ring the changes on their models: the heads, weapons, and even the top and bottom halves of the torsos are interchangeable, whilst belts are removable, and pistols can be drawn from their holsters and swords from their scabbards, thus opening up enormous opportunities.

A remarkable example, worth describing in detail, is their 'Wars of the Roses' set, comprising six foot and four mounted warriors, each in a different posture, with a choice of two realistic horses. The weapons consist of two types of swords (with separate scabbards and belts), battle-axe, lance, bill, crossbow with quiver, longbow with arrows, and misericord. There are eight distinct types of movable visors, and shields in eight styles (the red and white rose centre-bosses are anachronistic and unfortunate, as are the moulded designs). The trappings, cloths and ornamental bridles of the horses are detachable, as are the banners. It would be difficult to collect a full set of the varied crests which plug into the tops of the helmets, as different batches of models are sent to different firms for sale, and the following list may be incomplete: head of bull; mastiff; jester; swan; bear; pelican; horse passant; lion passant–regardant; lion crowned; phoenix; wyvern; cross; crescent; peacock's feathers; Prince of Wales' feather; bunch of feathers; pinnacle or crocket.

These are in either red or white. Finally, there are a number of mantlings and horse-trappings of differing design and colour. The general position of the models is reminiscent of the hollow-cast 'Knights of Agincourt'.

Another, inferior set, without the 'Swoppet' characteristics, and with paper-transfer banners and shields, issued in 1968, is a sad falling off from the generally high standard set by the firm, as found on the whole in their 'Deetail' range, first issued in 1971, with the feet slotted into metal stands, thus giving a more rigid balance to the model.

The 'Swoppet' principle was seized on eagerly by other firms, who grasped the idea but were lamentable in their application of it; their attempts have gradually faded out.

The only serious contender in popularity or skill is Model Soldiers (or Timpo), whose most successful efforts are West Point Cadets and vigorous mounted Cossacks. Their most ambitious effort (although not the most successful) is their 'Battle of Waterloo' set. It is a pity that a little more research was not made into details such as the colour of Napoleon's greatcoat, the shape of Blucher's cap, and the omission of Wellington's famous frock coat in favour of a gorgeous uniform, as the set is vigorous in its approach. Together with earlier sets, it sank into obscurity, but has recently been revived under the title of 'Action Pack' the only difference being that the models are unpainted. (One military modelling journal thought it was an entirely new production.) It will be noted with all Timpo models that the same basic horses are used irrespective of period (Roman, or Western, or Napoleonic) whereas Britains-Herald endeavours to vary the posture in different sets and suit the horses to the periods (and what beautiful horses they are!).

At one time one could purchase a fair range of Crescent products, including a set of 'Old Contemptibles', with a machine-gun and a mounted bugler, 'Mounties', and the French Foreign Legion; whilst Cherilea issued two sets of Romans (one 6cm size), Vikings, Saxons, Zulus, Arabs, the 8th Army, troops in the service of Henry of Navarre and of Wolfe, and Spanish Armada infantry. All were notable only for their violent action.

Undistinguishable from their competitors other than by the trademarks were Trojan and Speedwell, but Cavendish Miniatures set a new standard by the production of a boxed set of a yeoman warder of the Tower of London, a trooper of the Household Cavalry and a London policeman. They followed this with a fine set of four figures of the 1758 period (designed by Stadden) which were of outstanding quality (although the paint flaked off easily). Apart from a distinguished set of Henry VIII and his wives (again designed by Stadden) the firm has added nothing further, which is to be regretted, as all the models are worthy of preservation.

Many of the British plastic models were pirated in Hong Kong, and some terrible results were to be seen and to be forgotten as soon as possible. One enthusiast, however, James Opie, made it his task to acquire specimens of everything, however repulsive, and to preserve them in their original boxes or plastic containers; whilst many weird and ridiculous specimens went into his bag, at the same time he conducted his own researches into the productions in plastic of those makers who had originally issued their models in hollow-cast.

The nearest equivalent to the British alkathene model is that of Louis Marx, of the United States. As prolific as Heyde, they have made sets of models nowhere else obtainable, including Roman circuses with many civilian figures, fairy-tale characters and the like, mostly of a uniformly high quality. They were usually issued in large sets in several sizes, and up to about ten years ago were usually available in Woolworths' stores in Great Britain, but with the rise of Britains-Herald and the competition from other types of plastic models, they appear to have vanished from the market.

Spain, also, in the form of Reamsa, have issued attractive sets. The best of these, designed by George Erik, late of Wimbledon, are a Roman chariot, medieval warriors, and a set of the French in Spain. The figures based on the film *El Cid* are a curious mixture. The foot models of the Christians and the Infidels show a lively imagination, but the mounted troops display a wanton disregard for chronology. In fact, the riders (quite attractive) are new models placed astride horses designed years ago in the whole realm of chivalric fantasy. Other similar models are marketed under such titles as 'Ricardo Corazon de Leon' and 'Caballeros del Rey Arturo' and show the same indifference to period. A set of bull-fighters, however, each a portrait-model, is in a different class.

Italy is also a prolific producer of alkathene models, the majority being of large size and execrable style. The best bear the trademark of a ten-gallon hat (we are unable to identify the maker), and others are by Mardi and T.B.S., whilst a set (obtainable in England at the time of writing) of fourteenth- to fifteenth-century armour specimens in 60 and 120mm are attractive, though not equalled by Vikings in the same sizes from the same anonymous firm.

The type of plastic more common on the Continent in general is of a harder composition, not readily described. The main characteristic is rigidity and a somewhat metallic feeling. The chief manufacturers are Merten (Berliner Plastichen Composition), and Hausser (Elastolin). The former has a wide range of 40 and 54mm models, including modern troops, landschnechts, civilians and medieval fighting men, including archers and assault troops, scaling ladders and siege weapons. Cavalrymen are detachable from about six basic horses, and weapons are made of polystyrene.

Elastolin models are probably the best known of any type of material after Britains, Heyde and Mignot. Before World War II they were large and clumsy, made of a type of mixed sawdust, resin and glue, built round a wire armature. One knock and a piece fell off. They had, it is true, no pretensions to be anything but toys, but there appears to be an eager collecting-public for them. Like Heyde, they produced large sets, including transport, pontoon bridges, and the like. These have recently been revived. A rarity is a complete set of Hitler and his henchmen. Their greatest competitor, Lineol, whilst having as large a range, produced models of infinitely greater quality, as a comparison between their Hindenburg and the Elastolin Hitler will amply show.

After their plant was bombed at the end of World War II, Elastolin turned to other methods of production, and at the same time changed their designs so that today they are among the most skilful of large composition figures, and their new ranges are eagerly sought for by collectors. The material of which they are made, akin to polystyrene, enables the designer to undercut and give far more detail than was previously possible. The colour appears to be integral to the material.

Their Romans are perhaps the most popular venture, although a more recent series of landschnechts displays this brutal period in all its savage finery. Indeed, there is an element of sadism in many of the models, especially those of the Huns and the Vikings. Far more acceptable to some people are the medieval 'Prince Valiant' models, of no recognisable period other than a generalisation of the tenth century. The large size of the models makes them difficult to assimilate, and far more preferable is the 40mm range, scaled down exactly from the larger counterparts. However, the price of both sizes seems excessive.

Of the French makers, those of Starlux are undoubtedly the most attractive. The larger models are 56mm in height and are distinguished by excellent moulding and colouring. There is also a 35mm range. Obtainable are chasseurs alpines, marines, parachutists, legionaires, Algerians, Westerners and Indians, Mexicans, corsairs, etc, together with splendid Romans and some of the most attractive medieval models ever made, especially those of females. The only models so far available in England are those of the Napoleonic army, a wide range including many cavalry units. They cannot, however, be said to come up to the standard of the models representing the earlier periods.Other French makers are Clairet, JIM, Guilbert, and, in 40mm, MDM, whose First Empire troops may be seen in the foyer of many a French hotel.

Two other remarkable ventures must be mentioned, although the models are obtainable only by the purchase of tins of coffee. One is Mokarex, of Paris, the other Café Storme, of Mouscron, Belgium. Both are in the same tinny type of hollow plastic, and issued unpainted in a dull metallic colour. Both explore the complete range of history from the earliest times, the one of France, the other of Belgium, and civilians figure largely in both series. In both, some of the models are exquisite, whilst others are not up to normal standard. The horses especially are badly scaled. (The riders are made separately.) The Mokarex models are all in one piece, but certain of those of Café Storme have separate heads, legs and arms, and a magazine is issued explaining and illustrating how conversions may be made. Figures in both series reach to over three-hundred, and they must indeed have promoted the sale of coffee. Lest one is inclined to think that undue attention is being paid to what are after all 'giveaways' comparable to those found occasionally in cornflake packets, it is instructive to know that from 1965 to the last model issued in 1969, the firm of Historex and their designer Eugène Lelièpvre were concerned in the production of Café Storme models, whilst for Mokarex, Monsieur M. Leroux designed the figures from 1958 to 1964, to be succeeded until 1967 by Lelièpvre. The best of the models warrant good painting, and when complete compare favourably with metal figures. English counterparts have been urged for years to issue a comparable collection, but all that has recently appeared is a 40mm semi-solid plastic group of mixed periods and too flexible weapons which do less than justice to the designer.

The tremendous present-day interest in World War II and the activities of the antagonists has manifested itself mainly in the polystyrene kit of armoured fighting vehicles following in the tradition of the aircraft kits which have proved so popular. There are now innumerable firms turning out an incredible and increasing variety of guns, tanks, waggons, jeeps, motorcycles and the like, with the result that an increasingly large number of collectors are assembling complete modern armies down to the last detail. From a psychologist's point of view it is perhaps interesting to note that the main producer of these replicas of mechanised warfare are the Japanese, and the names Tamiya and Fujima are seen in every model-shop throughout the world.

These vehicles and armaments, naturally, have to have crews to go with them, and the Japanese in particular are satisfying this demand. Usually in groups of five or six men in differing postures, they are designed in alkathene for their specific purpose but not always in correct scale. It is here that the mathematician has to take over, as the armoured vehicle kit enthusiast talks of 1/32nd and the like, whereas the model-soldier collector is more at home in millimetres. It is time that the manufacturers of both got together and made up their minds as to a foolproof nomenclature. The difference of approach with these plastic models is that whereas the collector of model soldiers per se looks at a model as an individual piece, the armour enthusiast buys his as a means to an end, with an eye to what conversions may be undertaken to turn, for instance, an Afrika Korps man into a Britisher, and vice versa.

Lest it be thought that alkathene has been confined to the production of cheap, mass-produced models, good though some may be, it should be mentioned that John Niblett has issued a 54mm gold-plated Robert the Bruce, based on the 17ft high granite statue by Pilkington Jackson. At £1.35 ($4.50) this is expensive. Even more so is the equestrian model made for the Tower of London (£2.25) ($6) larger in size, and of much better design and execution. There is also a series in strict 54mm of reproductions of Spanish armour, made for the Réale Armoria of Madrid, where the alkathene is of some harder and more metallic material, and simulated to represent age and wear.

9

THE POLYSTYRENE REVOLUTION

About 1947 a firm in Deal began making a series of compressed 54mm plastic models which were marketed under the name of Malleable Mouldings. The significance of this firm is that they were the first in England to mould arms, heads, legs and weapons in separate pieces and then assemble them to the torso. The result was a sound, competent model with little chance of viability, and, despite the efforts of Henry Harris the firm had to close down. Although the models were sold assembled, the germ of future developments was there, but nobody spotted it for years. Malleable Mouldings are now quite rare, especially when cast in metal, as was done with a few special models, at the request of collectors.

A tiny, unique venture in making a polystyrene model in two pieces, assembled and mounted on a base, was made by an obscure firm called Rogard, operating from the fastnesses of Wales. It apparently met with no success, and was probably intended for the souvenir trade. However, it was a precursor of things to come.

The introduction in 1957 of large polystyrene kits in several pieces by Aurora of the United States began a fashion of self-assembled models. These large productions, a series of models of famous armour, well-designed and made, and easy to assemble and paint, appealed immediately to young and old alike. The shining silvered, blued or blackened armour, with gold lines painted on by the purchaser, on its simulated marble plinth, certainly looked most attractive on the mantelpiece or in the hotel foyer. The idea was immediately expanded by the introduction of mounted models culminating in a 'Gold Knight'. These kits were in several large pieces, and assembled by means of a special liquid which, if not sparingly used, cemented the modeller to the statuette.

The idea was taken up by the English firm Selcol, who issued two much more elaborate and attractive models of Elizabeth I and Richard I, designed by E. Meister, which taxed the assemblers ingenuity and understanding of costume. Unfortunately they were immediately challenged by Airfix with a smaller, cheaper and inferior model. These had, and still have, a wide following. Quite a number of kits are available, of which the best are the Black Prince (although his shield could never be lifted), the worst an impossibly insipid Joan of Arc to whom nobody would have paid the slightest attention, and the most popular a Guards infantryman.

In France the firm of Segom had about 1950 developed the Malleable Mouldings idea, also in 54mm, but in a type of polystyrene. Issued unassembled, their figures were not particularly well designed, however, having a pronounced anatomical quirk. They concentrated on the troops of France from the seventeenth to the nineteenth century, and whilst highly regarded in France, were little-known in other countries, except by those enthusiasts who collected Irish troops in the service of France, the 'Wild Geese'. Collectors accustomed to metal models did not quite know how to overcome the difficulties encountered in painting on an alien surface, the result in many cases resembling rather badly-glazed porcelain.

However, when M. Biéville took over a few years ago, the quality increased enormously, and they are now a most attractive collection, constantly being added to. Basically a model consists of a simple torso; the arms, head, uniform and accessories are stuck on, whilst from the waist downwards the buttocks, thighs and legs are in one piece. Many variations of figure may be achieved, and spare parts are purchasable. An unusual feature is that the trimming of the hats of certain ranks of the army of the Capets is of simulated lace. When assembly has been completed the creamy plastic surface is attractive even if not painted.

In 1964 a new firm emerged whose name, Historex S.A., must be reckoned as important historically as that of Hilpert, Lucotte, Heyde and Britains. Eugène Lelièpvre, with whom I had been in correspondence for some time, wrote to me enthusiastically about the new venture, in which he was engaged on the designs, and sent me an advance model long before the project was announced to the public. I was confronted by a mass of about sixty different pieces of white polystyrene, all attached to sprues, and searched in vain for assembly instructions, even though an illustration and colour guide were provided.

I managed fairly successfully to assemble the horse, add the saddle-cloth and the saddle, put the two halves of the rider together, add the head, the arms, and the pelisse, only to become bogged down with the terrible array of 'overs'. Should this go here? Where does this piece go? And so it went on, by trial and error, and fraying of temper, and a superfluity of liquid cement. At last something approximating to the maker's original intention emerged, only for fresh difficulties to be encountered over the painting. I never did finish it, and I have no idea where it is now. This was something new, something perhaps alien to my conception of to what limits collectors should go, allied to which my manual dexterity with tiny objects and quick-flowing adhesive was extremely limited.

When I first wrote about Historex I recognised that, although the models were far more expensive than anything else on the market apart from painted models, something new was emerging that might influence collecting. I had no inkling of the tremendous impact that Historex would have. In a flash, in the twinkling of an eye, 'do-it-yourself' had arrived, and with it a new generation of collectors, calling themselves 'model-makers' but more truly assemblers. Now, given dexterity, patience in sorting the components, skill in cutting the bridles, ability to cement and not be cemented, was a way of imagining that one was creating an original model. It was as if the frustrated attempts at painting in oils had turned the enthusiast to a 'painting by numbers' set. The original picture had been designed by a professional, the outlines of areas drawn carefully and lithographed with numbers onto already prepared canvas, the colours supplied in a handy box, together with brushes and turpentine and medium, and a list of colours corresponding to the numbers worked out. All one had to do was to follow the instructions, frame the result when dry, and hey presto! – instant painting! No need to go through the labour of learning to draw, even. Similarly the model enthusiast now had a polystyrene model, the result of hours of thought and the making of innumerable sketches by a military expert, anatomically and historically correct, down to the most minute detail, obligingly dissected ready for him to assemble. All he had to do was to follow the instructions (if there were any) mount the result when dry, and hey presto! – instant modelling! No need to go through the labour of learning to draw, how to work clay or plasticine, to make a mould and cast the metal.

A pleasant enough pastime, one would have thought, but the cult has now grown to a mania. No longer are the results confined to august and traditional gatherings of model-soldier societies, but they now figure in such once unthought-of fields such as the gatherings of the International Plastic Modellers and the Model Engineering ranks, to take their places among aeronautical and marine kits.

Now that I have, I hope, placed them in their true perspective, I must add that in many instances the results are quite astonishing. It appears that the world was just waiting for these kits, and for Napoleon and his armies in particular. For it is to the armies of his era that Historex is at the moment dedicated, and every month that goes by shows an additional offering. Practically every unit has been, or is to be, represented, and presumably if and when this has been achieved the firm may look backwards into history. (Actually in 1973 they looked forward to World War II – with German troops.) It has also recently concerned itself with a token representation of the British Army of the period, and, of all things, a Lady Godiva. Time alone will reveal what more Messieurs Lelièpvre and Gillet have up their sleeves.

It is interesting to trace the history of the acceptance of Historex in England. Although they were first imported in 1965, their first advertisement was not to appear in an English journal until February 1966, and the first mention of their appearance at an exhibition was in the *Bulletin* of the British Model Soldier Society in August the same year:

> Nobody who attended the Annual Competition this year can have missed the excellent set piece of Napoleon and Horse Grenadiers of the Guard. These were Historex figures beautifully painted by a member of the Society and it took very close examination to establish that they were plastic figures. . . . Designs for Historex are by Eugène Lelièpvre, the famous French military painter. No wonder they are so good.

In October in the same year a group received mention at an exhibition in the north of England, and the first article on converting them was issued in April in the following year. In a questionnaire of collectors' interests made in 1968 not a single member of the British Model Soldier Society is recorded as being interested, but by June 1969 they were creeping into competitions as conversions, whilst in April 1970 the British Society's annual exhibition was graced by Lelièpvre himself. The final accolade was given when in April 1971, the annual competition included a Historex trophy for the first time.

Other makers were quick to follow in the footsteps of Historex. Prairial, for example, produced a few models of the same period, including eight versions of Wellington, four on foot and four mounted. Riders were supplied in one pack together with the horse furniture, the horses in another. Assembly and painting instructions were provided. Airfix, having had the

Page 105 (*above*) Small-size models are becoming increasingly popular. Those made by Edward Surén (Willie) are of splendid quality; (*centre*) Super smalls: the small-size products of a number of makers are worthy of separate display. In this assembly of 20, 25, 30 and 40mm models the works of the following are shown: back row: Stadden (2), Elastolin (plastic), Minot, Stadden. Front row: Eriksson, Higgins, Stadden, Greenwood & Ball (diorama figure), Higgins, Eriksson (3), Niblett (group); (*below*) Historic flats: Heinrichsen was famous for his large sets. Here is a small selection, in the original painting, of a country market group.

Page 106 (*above*) Smaller still: these unpainted models are of high quality, and by Silvercross, Thomas, Douglas and Hinchliffe. The smaller ones (painted, 15mm) are by Laing, whilst the real 'tinies' in the foreground are by Heroics (6mm); (*below*) Medieval battle (solids): 30mm models by Eriksson, Lamming, Miniature Figurines and Garrison.

monopoly of the market for 20mm wargame figures in 1972 launched into the 54mm size in polystyrene, beginning with a Coldstream Guardsman, a trooper of the 10th Regiment of Hussars, and a trooper of the Scots Greys, the former in an 'at ease' position, the two mounted models in animated action. Their kits are not nearly so elaborate as those of Historex, there being about thirty-five pieces to each of the mounted ones, and the price is phenomenally low. As is to be expected, they have been seized upon with avidity by the converters, and immediately used in conjunction with their French counterparts.

In 1970 Dennis Knight announced that despairing of attempting to find models of the same scale and period at reasonable prices, he intended to design and market his own. Thus Helmet Products was born. The principle is the same, in that various parts have to be assembled, but although the material looks like polystyrene, it is a special PVC plastic, which, claims Mr Knight, carves and sandpapers much more easily. It is, however, necessary to use Helmet's own special adhesive and undercoating. Needless to say, the kits are so far (with only one exception) of the ubiquitous Napoleonic wars, and they are certainly a welcome addition, especially at their very reasonable price. Designed by David Pomeroy, interesting features are that metal parts are already plated, and wool and fibre items included. The thick, alkathene-like bases, however, detract from the completed result.

10

MISCELLANEA

Representations of military figures have been made in many materials other than metal or plastic, although today they are rarely favoured by commercial manufacturers, who, naturally, have their livings to make. However, it would be a pity if they were neglected, as one can still occasionally come across interesting specimens in museums or antique shops.

The most obvious material is clay, its use dating back to early classical times, and extending through the Middle Ages (especially in Central Europe) right through to the present day. Owing to its fragility many models must have perished. Allied to clay is plaster, which found expression mainly in the late nineteenth century when it was used mostly for large presentation or commemorative purposes, such as an equestrian model of Major General Williams, 'the hero of Kars'. Papier-mâché, (or carton comprimé) has the same inherent defects as plaster, its friability; but even so it had a vogue, especially in France, at the end of the nineteenth century, when certain 5 or 6in-high French troops mounted on springs were extremely popular. Thousands must obviously have vanished, as they were mostly made for boys.

Wood is a vehicle that has been much used for model soldiers, sometimes by itself, at other times as a basis for the building-up of other materials. In the past there was a considerable native industry among the country populations of most countries, when the long winter evenings could be turned to profitable account. Inevitably there was not much skill or variety to be expected, but that there was a ready market for large or small infantry and cavalry, having merely an approximation to accuracy of uniform, is shown by literary references, contemporary illustrations, and by the illustrated catalogues of German dealers in toys, where forts and castles are also shown, some with a pop-gun type of cannon. Folk-art apart, occasionally one sees a carving of extra quality, made, one would imagine, for the souvenir market, such as a group of 6in kings surrounding the tomb of Maximilian, or Joan of Arc with the *oriflamme*. The humble household peg and lathe-turned cotton reel have also been made, somewhat unexpectedly, into model soldiers, although these are merely ephemeral oddities which have their amusing side.

William Britain began business as a maker of mechanical toys, and the museum of the firm contains a few examples. These are of the money-box variety (black sambo conveying a coin to his mouth via his hand), and in two instances mechanical devices were introduced into his military figures: 'Soldiers to shoot' and an archer with target. Automata have been made from the earliest times, mainly in the form of clocks, but occasionally one may see a musical box decorated with moving military bandsmen. During the period when models were used for drill demonstration a number of types of automata were used, including the simplest of all, the trellis tongs. A more elaborate type consisted of a large box of 40mm solid models, in three trays, the top containing an elaborate assembly of slots into which the models were fitted, and then induced at the command of a switch to undergo evolutions. An amusing type of semi-automata is a Don Quixote who, with his limbs attached to his torso by springs, accordingly trembles violently when touched. It came from the United States. Even Berdou has made a model or two in which a cavalryman is mounted on a spring, so that movement is affected at the touch of a finger.

In the days before hollow-casts street vendors did a good business in models made of conjoint tin. These large, mass-produced crudities were made in two conjoint halves, mass-painted, and then clipped together with metal flanges. They lasted until the 1930s, and it is conceivable that the method of construction – a vacuum enclosed by two shapes – may have given Britain the germ of the idea for his hollow-casts. Another, still cheaper idea, was the use of compressed empty sardine tins, which, after cleaning and straightening, were cut by jigs into silhouette figures which were then printed in colours and supported by a turned-over footstand. The idea was revived by the Nazis when they issued thin metal figures in packets of cigarettes.

Paper sheets have an old and honourable history, and it would require a separate volume to attempt to describe their many facets. They were primarily intended to be hand painted, mounted on thin card, cut out and affixed to small blocks of wood. Collections are occasionally offered for sale or appear at auction (a complete auction sale was devoted to them in Germany in 1972, and a collection of nearly four-hundred sheets by Silbermann was sold at Sothebys in 1968). Examples of especially fine sets may be seen at the Musée Carnavalet in Paris (eighteenth century), at the San Marino Museum in Naples (nineteenth century), at the Leyden Museum (twentieth century) and the Musée at Strasbourg (a complete range). These sheets each contain a number of figures, and must not be confused with supplements in books. Italy and Spain in particular still issue large numbers of sheets, the majority being very crudely printed in colour, and there are instances of modern attempts at reviving fine quality illustrations, notably by Norman Newton Ltd and by Alan Robinson-Sagar in Canada.

A similar idea, in 30mm for diorama purposes, consisting of a small series of Napoleonic cavalry and British infantry squares, were drawn and published by René North, commencing about 1965, and continuing after his death in 1969. Curious Victorian and Edwardian offshoots may occasionally be seen, in which chromolithographed guardsmen with movable legs, or a combat group of two layers, connected with tape, form a three-dimensional picture. A collector should never neglect the opportunity of examining a scrapbook of this period – he might well find one of these or similar items, or, indeed, a complete Épinal or Nancy sheet.

The study of boxes and containers in which models are issued is in itself a rewarding subject. The earliest date from the time of mass production of flats. These tiny models were placed flat in shavings in oval boxes of the thinnest possible wood, with a handwritten label. With specialisation, these were replaced by cardboard boxes, each row of models separated by a strip of paper cut short so that the torso lay flat, the footstand thus lying free. The subject was then denoted in manuscript on the label, which now bore the maker's name printed upon it. This is still the standard method of packing flats. Solid models were issued in Germany in very stout cardboard boxes, the upper part of the lid highly decorated, and bearing the maker's name in gold, the indication of the quality of the models, and facsimiles of any medals that had been won. Finer quality models were contained in highly polished wooden boxes, with gilded lettering and embellishments.

Britains' early boxes bore a long descriptive label, usually with a drawing and sometimes the name of the artist (often that of Fred Whisstock). These boxes and their original contents are now much sought after. Each model was held in place at strategic parts by thread which passed through a hole in a sheet of white card. Later the firm accepted the changing times, and turned either to a more modern type of box, with the divisions for the figures moulded to their shape in plastic, or to an individual box with a transparent cover, a practice used nowadays by Greenwood & Ball and by Mignot. Mignot, however, for years issued flats and solids in shelved boxes with a diorama-type background. The American firm of Tru-Craft had a very strong glazed paper-covered squarish box, with a highly decorative design on the upper cover. Imrie-Risley's larger models have their own individual cardboard containers, but the majority of contemporary makers of metal models sell their products in the form of a transparent envelope.

Porcelain seems by its fragility and its lack of unified purpose to come outside the range of normal model-soldier collecting. The statuettes are undoubtedly a joy to behold, but their scope is limited to the adornment of a rich man's cabinet, irrespective of whether he is a collector of militaria. Just occasionally, however, an attempt at a logical sequence comes to one's notice, such as the new series projected by Lelièpvre and Rousselot, at present on sale at 'The Soldier Shop' in New York. Still confined to some dozen Napoleonic figures, the series may well reach serious proportions. Less to be recommended is a set of atrocious 3ft-high wall plaques advertised quite seriously for collectors, or the monstrous plastic imitations of metal warriors one sees in chain-stores.

Although chessmen need not necessarily be military figures, they form an attractive vehicle for the display of heraldry or uniform. One of the earliest known sets, the Lewis set, has been reproduced in plastic by the British Museum and also by another, commercial, company. Indian sets showing the troops of John Company and its native levies and opponents, and fearsome Chinese and Burmese warriors are traditional, especially in their use of the elephant, but a nineteenth-century set from Canton is unusual in that it has a very odd Napoleon as one of the kings. The French monarchs had most elaborate sets carved for them, including Hannibal and Scipio Africanus, the Battle of Tolbiac, between Clovis and Alaric, and the Battle of Agincourt. A seventeenth-century set from Holland depicts the pawns as twelfth-century men-at-arms and the knights as cavalrymen of the Thirty Years' War. Saracens and Crusaders have been portrayed many times, whilst one of the finest collections carved in the nineteenth century depicts personalities of the Austrian court of the sixteenth century and includes the figures of the kings guarding the tomb of Maximilian. Flaxman designed a notable set of classical warriors for Wedgwood in 1783, and another set in the same vein, this time in iron, was cast at Offenbach sur Maine in 1849.

Nearer our own times, a set in ivory, carved in 1937, depicts the struggle of Ethiopia and Italy, with the Italian rooks portrayed as tanks. Fouillé made a lovely set of sixteenth-century troops in 54mm, together with the board and the elaborate architectural setting, and in 1973 Surén announced an edition of twenty-five sets of the Battle of Pavia. Ping has made several, including Bannockburn and Crecy, and Hinton one of the American Revolution. One of the most famous collectors of chess sets, the late Colonel Thomas Sutton, designed and painted an Austerlitz, which was carved for him in wood by a Brighton workshop. With the moulding possibilities of plastic, a number of fine sets have become available. One can see a magnificent Joan of Arc set in Paris, and a less fine Seven Years' War has appeared in London and the provinces. Both are very expensive, but a Battle of Agincourt, designed in 45mm by Stadden for Triang, and beautifully (if at times erroneously) painted, is more reasonable in price. Unfortunately, in this particular set, the problem inherent in plastic, the bending of the lances, is in evidence.

11

MAKING AND CONVERTING

So far the models already discussed have in the main been made by professionals whose living is dependent on their sales. Economics being a prime factor for consideration, they are understandably reluctant to embark on new lines which may bring them much acclaim but little financial reward, and inevitably (unless they are in the fortunate position of working to commission only) they seek the easier and cheapest means of production, time being of paramount importance. It is they who are the solid base of the hobby. However, human nature as it is, they cannot attempt to please everybody, and there has been, and is, and ever shall be, the keen collector, who, whilst appreciating the efforts of the professional, and indeed applauding them, still remains unsatisfied. The urge to create predominates, and eventually finds its expression in its own way. Sometimes this results in a new entrant into the commercial field, at others a peaceful, creative existence.

In the past this urge was confined to a few individuals with leisure to spare who could in their own time experiment with materials as an agreeable pastime, the results being the subject of admiration and appraisal from a small band of fellow enthusiasts; but with the evolution of new materials this gentle pastime has become much more widespread. The necessity to create, satisfied for many by the metal and polystyrene kits which now flood the market, with all their new possibilities, remains unappeased. These craftsmen often display great skill and their models are a worthy record of their enthusiasm, erudition, and ability.

Their presence is felt at society exhibitions all over the world, but unless one attends every one of these (an obvious impossibility) inevitably many must remain unknown except to their own intimate circle. The advent of certain magazines, however, has brought their work before a much wider range of collectors, and it is strange indeed if each month a new maker is not featured. Even so, it is not every collector who purchases magazines, and it is not every maker who is reported upon. A maker of exquisite figurines in Vancouver, for example, known to all his Canadian colleagues, and possibly in the northern parts of the United States, may well be unheard of in Great Britain. Similarly, one whose models have aroused great interest in the Midlands may well be unknown in London except to travelling society members. One can therefore, only give a token list of such names as David Fordham, William Hearne, Peter Wilcox, Magnus Schreiber, and Ole Høyer, who, occasionally, will part with a model to their friends, if pressed, and whose efforts bring so much pleasure to others. There are certainly many others, but one is regretfully unable to give them the notice they undoubtedly deserve.

At one time the most popular material for making personal models was lead, or rather an amalgam of lead and a strengthening alloy, which is still occasionally used for a standard basic torso. The process of making a mould is complicated, and a description is best left to a professional model-maker. However, so many new materials are becoming available that in many cases the older method of a metal or silicone-rubber mould is now confined mainly to the professionals. A few collectors use this method to create a metal model complete with arms, legs and head, but no clothing or equipment, simply as a stock casting. Peter Wilcox, for example, in his superb portrayal of ancient and barbaric races, uses a self-designed model in 60mm, which he casts in batches of about forty at a time from silicone-rubber moulds. After cleaning the flash from the casting, it is then roughed up or 'keyed' for plaster by scoring with an old lino-cutting knife. It is then animated to the desired position and soldered to a base of brass or tin plate, and metal built up over the feet for the subsequent making of shoes or sandals. Then with an old brush Wilcox applies a thoroughly mixed superfine filling plaster, such as Crown, Polyfilla or Dulite, of a semi-stiff consistency. When dry the plaster is carved and 'attacked', as he calls it, in various ways to represent body hair, trousers, fur, tunics, cloaks, leather jerkins, sheepskin jackets and the like. Long cloaks are made in the traditional manner from sheet lead.

Belts, straps and slings are fashioned from thick art paper cut from the margins of glossy magazines, buckles and brooches are made from lead. For shoulder guards, plates and studs, Bristol board or sheet lead is either cut or punched out. Weapons consist of either actual material or commercially available ones are used. He finds that manufacturers' shields are normally too large or too thick, so he constructs them himself, often laminating them in a semi-cylindrical shape made in sections of boards and battens, sheet lead often being used. Precast helmets are incorporated when suitable, or carved from plaster and the surface carefully finished with flour paper. For mail, nylon is sometimes used, or built up with solder and then engraved. Priming is carried out with polyurethene-based eggshell finish for metal parts (apart from those left for burnishing), and emulsion paint for the figure.

Wilcox is certain that no deterioration will take place among this amalgam of media. He is a perfectionist, constantly experimenting in order to reach the apogee of texture and surface. Incidentally, he is not averse to using a commercially made horse upon which to build his own rider and equipment, and here the full armoury of the maker comes into use. (Similarly, Ping has recently made for me the first two models, the Knight and the Squire, of a projected set of the 'Canterbury Pilgrims', in which he features a horse which he designed at least twenty years ago, and has rarely cast since.)

A material one would hardly associate with model-soldier making is fibreglass resin, but there are at least two exponents of it, John Darnell and Pièrre Turner. The former makes his models in the traditional size, the latter in the larger 77 and 230mm. Darnell begins by carving his master figure direct from the material, whilst Turner makes an armless and legless torso of plasticine, plaster of paris, clay or modelling compound on a wire armature; the equipment and headgear are modelled separately. Then each makes a mould in two parts in the usual way, the material being a silicious-type rubber. When the mould is dry Turner mixes a small quantity of laminating fibreglass resin with a hardener and paints it on to the surface of the mould. When the resin has set, wire armatures are placed in the legs and arms and the mould closed and sealed. A further amount of resin is then mixed up and poured into the mould and left to set. The figure is then removed from the mould, cleaned, and the arms and headgear fitted to the body. Turner served for a few years with Russell Gammage, and then developed his own method of working. He confines himself to special commissions, and the quality of his work is apparent.

A Malcolm Dawson original 54mm model is born as a balsa-wood torso, with arm and leg attachments, not unlike an artist's lay figure without the ball and socket joints. To this framework he adds a head, hands and feet carved from Isopon. The whole is then covered with ordinary typing copy paper. The clothes are cut out separately, and each portion is rolled into a tight ball and then smoothed out again, to eliminate the stiffness of the paper. The pieces are then stuck to the basic figure with Copydex. When this operation is complete the whole is painted over with a solution of plastic sprue and Inhibisol or carbon tetrachloride, so that the details may be added from paper, stretched plastic sprue, plastic card or whatever else his ingenuity suggests.

The lasting quality of paper and card may be suspect, but this does not deter a number of makers, possibly because paper is so much easier to use than strips of metal, and even tissue paper can be pressed into service, as evinced by Stephen Turnbull, who concentrates on models of Samurai, where the intricate armour plates are built up on a self-cast original metal torso.

To the traditionalist it may appear even stranger to use plasticine pure and simple, but W. A. Thorburn was in the field as early as 1959 with a series of 12in models. More recently John Ciuffo has excelled in this particular material in 54mm models made mainly for museums. Whereas Thorburn coats his figures with a protective lacquer and subsequently paints them, Ciuffo uses a different coloured plasticine as required, thus reducing the necessity of painting, to a minimum. The only drawback apparent is that the resultant models must have the minimum of handling, and must perforce be kept in a glass case (individual models cost £6 each).

A much sturdier material that lends itself to the making of individual models is wood. The superb equestrian models of General Angenot are well known, as are the ones of an entirely different kind made by Pilkington Jackson. Arthur carved a number of large rather caricature-like models (continued in the same vein by his son), and Eriksson began his career by carving models of horses and riders. Don and Honey Ray, who in the 1930s were among the first makers in England of specialist 54mm metal models (they produced a large number on commission for Lord Greenway) are now making a name for themselves in Vancouver by their beautifully carved large models destined for museums. Particularly pleasant, also, although as yet little known in England, are the 54mm woodcarvings of the Italian Pranzetti.

In 1962 I received a visit from a collector who had just completed the carving of a copy of Niblett's plastic Robert the Bruce, but in larger size. It is interesting to know that Martin Rendall has progressed very greatly since those days, and has established himself as one of the leading carvers in the country. He has made a number of what he calls 'comic' knights (10in high) for Norman Newton Ltd, and more serious American Civil War and Napoleonic troops in the same size for Surén, as well as just completing a range of models from 1775 for an

American museum. He is also well known for his depiction of somewhat violent incidents at Agincourt. He favours limewood, which as a very fine grain and is satisfactory to carve. The painting is done in oils.

Plaster of all kinds has been used many times in the past, mostly for large models, those of the original Sentry Box, Willetts and Patmore (all in the 1960s) are well known. The nature of the material, however, limits both the output and the durability of the model, even though a metal armature is normally incorporated. Smaller (40mm) models have been made by Herbert Hahn and by Briton Rivière (Fabre, 54mm). In the United States Chuck Caldwell is turning out a long series of 150mm polychrome models in a plaster called 'Sculpy'. These apparently have a ready sale at quite high prices. Jack Cassin-Scott has made many models to commission, measuring anything up to 45cm. A plasticine master, strengthened by an aluminium armature, provides the basis for a series of separate parts which are assembled in a similar way to a kit. Moulds of plaster or rubber are used, and the model itself is made of a variety of materials, including metal and latex composition.

Indeed, there seems no end to the type of material used for the making of model soldiers, but not all of us are capable of seeing through the production of a figure from start to finish without relying on some form of aid afforded by an existing model. It is natural, therefore, that many attempts at conversion are made. To convert a model does not mean to bring a girl to religion, but in a sense the basis of the word is true – one dictionary puts it: 'to alter into something else'. To the collector of model soldiers it means one thing only – to turn any given model inside out.

There are many strata to conversion. The most obvious is the realignment of an arm or a head; the substitution of one weapon for another; the removal of minor articles of equipment or decoration; the placing of a rider on another horse. Taking a further step, a model may be sawn through its waist and the upper half of the torso allied to the lower portion of another model; if it is standing, it can be altered to a sitting position; or if its legs are splayed and bent at the hips it can be placed astride a horse. Possibly all that is required is a change of clothing or headgear.

To a certain extent the issue of so many models in kit form means that much of the simplest conversion, certainly of a metal figure, is unnecessary, as one can become one's own animator; but to the restless or ambitious this is mere chicken feed. Carrying the argument yet further, one might assume from the welter of new models pouring forth monthly from the makers' moulds that surely every period of history, every possible regiment and every conceivable position was more than adequately covered, but one attitude was expressed in a review of an armoured vehicle: 'To sum up, this is a nicely moulded kit without much conversion potential'.

Before the age of the plastic model the possibilites of conversion were restricted. The metal normally used in models was intractable, only those of Britains were at all easy to work. Any alterations had to be made with a small saw. The repositioning of an arm was achieved by cutting a notch in the inside of the elbow, bending the arm and filling the cut with either cold solder or plastic wood, or by using a soldering iron. If one possessed one of these it was possible to build on a torso such as made by Gammage, and many a conversion was effected by the use of the metal from an empty toothpaste tube, especially for banners and cloaks. Another method was to build up what was required with plasticine, apply liquid glue, and then coat with cold solder. This was perhaps the most effective: plastic wood never seemed to reach the required smoothness, however much it was sandpapered, and paint never seemed to lie so well on it.

The emergence of the polystyrene kit, however, revealed an extraordinary latent desire for self-expression. Some collectors are content enough to perhaps solder or glue an arm or two on a Gammage model, or to plug in the head so that it points in a different direction, and then to paint it most carefully and mount it appropriately. Now, however, this conception has been shattered by a wave of polystyrene-blooded collectors. One would perhaps have imagined that the assembly and painting of a Historex cavalryman, with the problems of correct order of gluing, the minutiae of buttons and medals and sword-knots and reins, would have satisfied the most exacting of purchasers. Far from it. There is a new, enquiring mind about, ever seeking something new, ever assessing a model for its potential to be turned into something entirely different from its original intention.

This new form of collector does not purchase his kit with the intention of making it as near to the maker's specification as possible. He stores it away, together with others, until the day that he decides that he would like a certain model in a certain pose. Out then come all the kits, and with the finished product either in the mind's eye or in illustration, he proceeds to review them with the idea of assessing the value of this horse's hind left quarter, or that horse's front right leg. Then he goes to another pack, and picks out a head, to another from which an arm is selected; he is not satisfied with the cavalryman at his disposal, but decides on an infantryman who can be sawn off at the waist, and then joined to the legs of a dismembered trooper. And so it goes on, until an entirely new model arises from the ruin of half a dozen kits. Nor does the modeller stop at Historex, but incorporates spare parts from other makes, plastic or metal, provided they are in the same scale.

The result of all this is a sensational display of ingenuity and considered calculation, which the creator may well claim as imaginative assembly. Certainly the results are sometimes amazing, especially when the modeller incorporates other material such as plastic card, plasticine or the improbable tissue or typing paper. One wonders about their permanency over the years. There is also the danger that the ingenious adaptor may be credited willy-nilly with the creation of an original work of art. Such a thing indeed happens, as when a certain well-known magazine which covers military model exhibitions referred to so-and-so's 'incredible model of a Hussar officer', failing to mention that it was based on two Historex kits, or when an extremely versatile and creative adaptor was figured on television in 'Collector's World' as 'model-maker extraordinary'. The culmination is reached when a collector can assert that, great as Berdou is, there are many collectors in the Midlands who turn out far better models.

Some of the results are undoubtedly magnificent, and should be recognised as specimens worthy of the highest praise. At the same time it should be said in fairness to those who conceive and execute their models from scratch, without recourse to prefabricated aids that the results should bear an inscription such as 'adapted from', or 'converted from' or 'based on', otherwise future historians will become bogged down under the impossible task of sorting out the original maker from the skilful adaptor. It is interesting to note that one American dealer does just this. In his 1972 catalogue he shows a number of Historex models, each of which is carefully labelled with the fact that they are conversions, giving the name of the converter. Incidentally, the esteem in which these amalgams are held is reflected in the fact that in one instance $150 (£35) is asked. It is a sobering thought that if one commissioned one of the great French makers to construct a unique equestrian model in lead it would not cost appreciably more.

With the advent of new plastic and other materials, the freedom of range became very much greater; but before examining this in detail it might be of service to mention the kind of equipment that a serious converter might be expected to require. First, a craft knife sold with four or five different blades, each for a particular use. Next, for metal figures, a small pencil-point soldering iron. A razor saw for amputation is essential, as are assorted files, scribers, engravers, razor blades, a pin vice, fine drills, blunt-ended pliers, a sharpening stone, sandpapers, and a pyrogravure for plastic kits.

Major Roy Dilly, a converter of long standing, lists in his book *Scale Model Soldiers* the following fillers and adhesives:

Page 123 (*above*) Wargame models: many of the wargame 25 and 30mm models produced today are worthy of careful individual painting. Top row: Hinton-Hunt (5), Rose (2), Higgins, Garrison, Miniature Figurines. Second row: Segom (2), Miniature Figurines (4), Warrior, Miniature Figurines. Third row: Garrison (6), Miniature Figurines (2). Foot: Alymer; (*below*) The large ones: larger size models present much scope for sculptural effects. These models are 90mm Men o'War, with the two in darker metal in 75mm by Lamb-Hinchliffe.

Page 124 (*above*) Series 77: Pat Bird is fast making a name for himself with his Series 77 larger models. The central model at the rear is by Cameron (120mm) and the two end figures in the front row are by Stadden (90mm); (*below*) Flats: an assembly of modern flats. Those in the background (by Rössner and Schweitzer) are in the traditional eighteenth-century size. The hawking party (from *Les Tres Riches Heures du Duc de Berri*) are by Hafer, whilst the figures of the Egyptian embalming scene were painted professionally on the Continent.

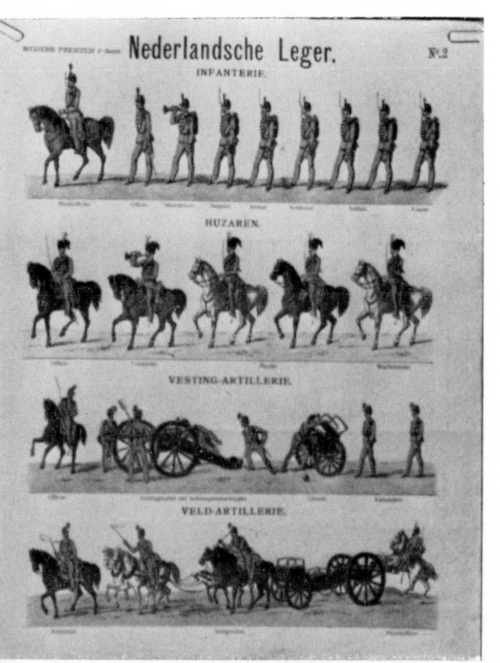

Page 125 Masterpieces of modern engraving: these modern flats exhibit all the characteristics of the more traditional showing the same vigour, excellence of production, skilful engraving and scrupulous historical accuracy. A number of 'combination' figures will be noted. Top row: Sivhed, Scholtz, Sivhed (3). Second row: Scholtz. Third row: Sivhed. Fourth row: Sivhed, Scholtz, Sivhed. Fifth row: Scholtz. Sixth row: Scholtz. Bottom left and right: Scholtz; Popular art: paper sheets of military uniform poured forth in profusion in France and Germany during the eighteenth and nineteenth centuries, to be quickly followed by printers in other countries. They are still issued in many European countries, but the present day designs are but a shadow of their predecessors. This sheet is by de Costa, Groningen, 1870–80 and shows Netherlands hussars and field artillery and comes from the superb collection of Cornelius Frazer of Amsterdam.

Page 126 (*above*) Revolutionary material: the polystyrene kits by Historex have provided a new dimension to the hobby. This group was assembled by the makers; (*below*) Conversion: enthusiasts of Historex kits are equally enthusiastic about converting them, as is seen in this group by C. Milani-Gallieni.

plastic card (plastikard), microstrip, Milliput, Isopon, plastic putty, greenstuff, cored solder, brass or copper shim, household or architect's pins, fuse wire, polystyrene cement, UHU, Mek-pac, liquid cement, Araldite, Unibond. To these could be added piano wire, a paper punch, linen, gauze, tissue paper, typing paper, plastic wood, Polyfilla – indeed, the list is endless, and one's own ingenuity will discover just the right otherwise-useless article for the job in hand. It will be noted that many of the above aids were issued originally for the re-creators of armoured fighting vehicle kits, and have spread through the whole world of conversion.

It would be tedious to describe the uses to which all these materials may be put; there are, after all, many roads to the same goal. It is, however, useful to know (and here we quote once more from Major Dilly) that plastic card is made in different thicknesses; that Isopon, which has a creamy consistency, can be built up over complete areas on metal to which it adheres extremely well if properly keyed beforehand, or can be pasted over tissue paper, cloth or other porous material for stiffening; it is hence especially useful for cloaks or the creation of feminine clothing, but is not satisfactory on plastic figures. Milliput is a putty-like plasticine, which hardens in two to three hours, and plastic filler, semi-liquid, can be used on polystyrene, where it is useful for filling up cracks and joins, and for building up in successive layers.

The firm of Segom, pioneers in the plastic kit, issue a most useful and refreshingly humorous handbook entitled *How to Animate Miniatures*. They call the material of their kits cellulose acetate. For the general assembly they recommend the use of either a glue made from an acetone base, a cement made for the repair of stoneware, or, better still, the acetate paste. This is made by dissolving pieces of the sprue in acetone, which is then pasted on the components. The acetone contained in the paste dissolves just sufficient of the acetate of the parts so that not only is a rigid bond created but it acts as a simultaneous welder and filler. For conversion, metal and other material can be incorporated permanently by using this adhesive in a thinner solution.

By a strange quirk, Segom's original kits did not attract much attention, but, by an even stranger coincidence, just as Britains' hollow-cast era was running out, to the dismay of the converters of metal models, Historex appeared on the scene with their new kits, which, whilst not exactly a new idea, far exceeded those of Segom in elaboration. The assembly of a single beautiful model was simply a matter of patience and manual dexterity and skill with polystyrene cement and colours. To those collectors who are content with a model as its designer intended, it may have appeared strange that this invention was to prove the most profitable vehicle for the display of the pyrotechnics of conversion.

Soon after Lelièpvre's designs for Historex appeared in this country, one of the former adherents of the metal model wrote in a society journal admitting his conversion to the new faith, and passed on some hints on how to set about assembling a basic kit. To begin with, polystyrene cement was squeezed on to a board, with cocktail sticks ready to hand so that the bare minimum of adhesive might be applied. The large areas of the model (in this case a cavalryman) were dealt with first, the halves of the body coated with cement and forced well together. Any cement that oozed out was shaved off when completely dry. The arms were next joined to the body, the body to the saddle and the rest of the equipment added, until the final stage of finishing off with the details of grenades, decoration of the turnbacks, medals etc, was reached. It was recommended that these tiny objects should be picked up on the end of a thin blade, or with a pair of tweezers. Cords on bearskins and shakos were bent before fixing; reins and slings were of the material supplied (although some prefer to use other materials) whilst for straps that are immobile it was suggested that plastic card was a more suitable substance. This completed the assembly of the kit, and painting followed (again, some prefer to paint the parts separately as they go along).

To alter a model one can adopt the traditional method of cutting a v-shape where required, bending back the affected limb, and recementing or filling with plastic putty or green-stuff. Another method is to use a pyrogravure. This is similar to a soldering iron which allows a small but constant flow of heat through the metal point. The tip is applied to the back of the knee or the elbow, the limb is pulled into the required position and realigned with ease where the plastic has become molten at the point of impact with the tip of the pyrogravure. The same tool will melt spare pieces of plastic sprue, so that the resultant material may be used for the filling up of v-cuts and joints, and will also roughen up bearskins, alter the design of a horse's mane, tail, mouth or ears: indeed, it is an essential tool for advanced work.

An example of a Historex conversion to something quite remote from the Napoleonic times is afforded by a Bugler of the 5th (Royal Irish) Lancers, created by William Hearne after a drawing by Caton Woodville. In this case pieces from four separate and distinctly different kits were used for the horse; and a single dragoon, drastically altered, served for the bugler. The rest of the model was self-made. The result would baffle anyone who attempted to discover the basic elements. Hearne has been featured many times in model magazines, and he and others similarly worthy have given a new dimension to the hobby.

Another enthusiast, Terry Beddis, remade a mounted figure of a Napoleonic camel corps in Egypt in the course of an evening. Upon a Britains' camel he placed a more suitable saddle and blanket made from plastic card, and then sat upon them a Historex hussar, making only a few substitutions: a right arm from a drummer, a bicorne hat from another model, weapons and stirrups from further kits, whilst the only other addition was a set of reins made from nylon thread.

These are examples of conversions involving the building of a single figure, but model adaptors today are much more adventurous. It would appear that the appetite feeds on itself, for no longer is the enthusiast content with the single model, but requires to exercise his skill on a group. Nolan Khan, for example, decided to make a 'Retreat from Moscow', but was sensible enough to restrict his vision to a few selected examples. Here only a few kits were used, and concentration directed to making drastic alterations to horse, rider and infantryman (three figures were planned) involving the 'tearing' of trousers, the replacement of inappropriate headgear, the adding of fuse wire chinstraps, special buttons, and cloaks of paper tissue stiffened against the icy wind by a liberal application of plastic solution.

The most startling transformation that it has been my fortune to see is a medieval group by Raymond Anderson. For some years he has been creating his own models by carving direct from polystyrene, and has been featured in a number of American magazines under the title he gives his workshop 'Western Dioramas'. Here, however, he used Historex kits for the creation of the 'Consecration of John of Gaunt'. The knight is kneeling before the Archbishop, and wearing a long cloak held by a page. At the right is a mailed supporter, whilst acolytes hover round the priest. In the background is a canopied effigy of a recumbent knight, whilst the altar is furnished with holy vessels. The only clue that one might have of the ancestry of one of the models is that the Archbishop resembles Napoleon. The whole scene is marvellously constructed and painted, and displays an imagination far above the normal.

It is disturbing to turn from this to another aspect of imaginative creating. A factor which is manifesting itself is the tendency to portray violence to the point of sadism in some of the models recently made or assembled. Personally I feel that it is a degradation of the use of materials, but, of course, I may be entirely alone in this view (although I suspect that certain of my more mild-mannered and gentler colleagues would agree with me). The facile answer which is given to every protest against violence or the lowering of any standard of morality is that we live in a violent age, which is reflected by its portrayers.

War is savage, brutal and inhuman, as periodically portrayed at the cinema and on the television. A film, however, is seen for an instant, shuddered at, and possibly forgotten quite soon afterwards. The details of carnage as depicted by contemporaries in Anthony Brett-James's *Europe against Napoleon* (an account of the Leipzig campaign) are revolting enough, but we have become accustomed to brutality in print. A model, however, is frozen in time, and is displayed in isolation. It seems, therefore, that a modeller must consider his subject very carefully before he begins it. I cannot think how a skilled converter could conceive, over many hours of cold-blooded thought and painstaking work a subject which is eventually to portray a French cavalryman in the actual moment of death, pierced by a sabre, which remains suspended in his lungs for the greater horror, whilst his bleeding hands vainly endeavour to remove the weapon. A model of this kind seems to me to be so vulgar that it can only do the hobby a disservice. The same apologists put forward the argument that such models are an indictment of war, and do much to counteract the influence of brilliant parade figures. The savagery of a Picasso or a Goya or a Callot is a cry from the heart of all humanity, and I cannot credit that the creators of violence in model-soldiers have this noble sentiment in their minds. As for my own position, it is akin to that of Faramir in Tolkien's *The Lord of the Rings*: 'I do not love the bright sword for its sharpness, nor the arrow for its swiftness, nor the warrior for his glory. I love only that which they defend.'

One of the most complicated and impressive groups of converted Historex kits is a re-creation by Cèsar Milani-Gallieni of the charge of the Scots Greys at Waterloo. Not content with a group of Stadden's 30mm models, he pictured the result in terms of larger dimensions, and to it he brought the full battery of the converter's aids: heated plastic sprue, dissolved plastic, plastic card, plastic rod, plastic carved with a knife, plastic carved with a pyrogravure, linen coated with a solution of dissolved sprue, stretched sprue for reins, plastic solution for chest padding, nylon cords for manes and tails. He thought first of making his own horses, which troubled him somewhat, but Historex arrived, and the advent of the Greys kit solved this problem.

Realising suddenly that there was an exhibition six weeks ahead, at which he wished to show an example of his work, he decided that it had to be now or never. His first conception was a group of nine troopers galloping abreast behind an officer, each, naturally, in a different posture. So horses were severed and joined again, involving the removal of fetlocks, knees and hooves for their new positions, muscles reshaped and reworked, and not only necks but mouths cut about and altered (Airfix heads were also amalgamated). He then turned to the riders, and subjected them also to being literally sawn apart, even to the fingers and the facial expressions. Painted and ready for the diorama work, he placed them in position and saw with dismay how empty the scene appeared. Deciding that at least another five men were necessary, he went to work again, cutting and filing and scalpeling, adjusting positions and painting the newly assembled figures. They were all then mounted on a diorama board, and simulated earth added. Still there appeared a hiatus, and long and careful study from every angle revealed a corner where a falling figure might well supply the balance needed. And so it proved. By working far into the night for six weeks he finished the model just in time. For the fifteen men and horses a proportionate number of kits was used, truly a mammoth operation.

As a contrast to this sustained and frenzied effort, a leisurely essay by Hearne took two years, off and on, to complete. He, like many other converters, is particularly gifted in amalgamating parts from metal and other models. The subject was a sergeant of the Arab Legion on desert patrol, the camel being an Elastolin model, much 'roughed up' by the pyrogravure. The man himself was carved from thick laminated plastic card, the uniform made from tissue paper coated with tube plastic cement and chloroform, and the head that of an Airfix hussar.

Dozens of tassels were made from suspension cords; and various other oddments such as dress-making tape, sellotape, fuse wire, nylon and bamboo were used.

There seems no limit to the adventurous mind, and there are seemingly endless possibilities of new worlds to conquer.

12

PAINTING

The quality of any model soldier depends primarily on the skill with which it is made, together with correct anatomy, accuracy of period, and general artistic conception, but all these remain unrealised until the final clothing in colour has been achieved. A poor model may be enhanced by fine painting, and equally a fine model can easily be spoiled by careless or incompetent handling of paint.

A number of makers will not sell their models exclusively as castings. They feel quite naturally that as they conceived the figure in the first place, and saw it through all its stages, it is right that they should finish it themselves. This applies not only to the specially commissioned model, but to those which are placed with agents for sale. Thus, to Courtenay and Ping and Greenwood, it would be inconceivable to allow someone else to paint the results of their skill. Stadden and Gammage originally adhered to this practice, until as their reputation grew it became impossible to maintain.

For the average collector the unpainted casting is possibly both desirable so that he may exercise his own skill, and necessary owing to the price difference. A 40mm mounted knight, for example, is available as a casting for £2.50 ($6.25), but is £5.50 ($14) painted and gilded. A 90mm model at £2.50 becomes £9 ($23) when painted by the journeyman. A 30mm flat, available as a cast at 20p costs the equivalent of £2.50 when painted, a wargame figure at 10p becomes £1.50 ($4) painted, whilst a 54mm model, primed ready for colour, and selling at prices varying between 90p and £2.50 is priced at three to four times this sum when painted.

Many makers are acutely conscious of the need of the collector to both keep a watch on his pocket and at the same time to be able to express himself. To those collectors who are not skilled in the arts of creation, and whose budgets are limited, there is nothing more satisfying than to exercise their skills with the brush. The result is, after all, what they themselves make it.

Before painting is commenced, it is advisable to undertake a few preliminary precautions, otherwise disappointment may be the result. A number of makers are careful to remove metal flash before marketing their models: others, alas, are extremely careless in this respect, so that at times quite a lot of work has to be done. Flash is particularly noticeable at the joins of the mould, especially in plastics; other vulnerable places are under the arms, between the legs, the reins, and the horse's head, right along the length of a lance, a sword or a scabbard, inside the sword hilt, and on various parts of mechanised weapons. Particularly infuriating is the model which arrives with thick metal pegs protruding from the soles of the feet and a thin metal base with no corresponding holes. Small amounts of flash can usually be removed quite easily with a sharp knife or craft blade, larger quantities may need drilling, filing and sand-papering. There is a tendency with alkathene for the surface to become frayed, but polystyrene is easily cut and can also be carved.

It may be necessary to fill up irregularities or gaps in the joins of the arms and other parts. This can be achieved with the aid of plastic padding, solder or cold solder, which, however, has a tendency to shrink, or plastic wood, which has the same defect. Any repair should, of course, be carefully filed down when the material has set. (As a matter of interest, and as an example of how far a connoisseur will go in the quest for perfection, I know of one such who disassembles any animated model he purchases on principle, and reanimates it himself.

Few of us would, perhaps, be so hyper-critical or so lacking in confidence in a chosen model or its maker.)

With metal figures it is advisable after the preliminary attention to immerse them in warm water to which has been added any ordinary washing-up powder. When dry an undercoat has to be applied, although there are some makers who do this for you. Examples of those in use are perfectly normal household emulsion paint (undercoat), titanium white (oils), Humbrol matt white, artist's gold size, or even vinegar. Personal preference should predominate. The only thing perhaps that might be noted is that whatever substance is applied it should be done very thinly, otherwise moulded or engraved detail may be obscured. This applies especially to flats.

Any model smaller than 54mm should be lightly stuck on to a piece of wood, to which is attached a handle in the form of a block. This block should be made so that it can stand upright at the end of a session, so that nothing can touch the possibly still-wet models. The length of wood depends entirely on the painter – a handy size is one that will take about half a dozen flats or 20mm models with sufficient space between each so that no awkward feeling about with the brush is necessary. Larger models may be mounted on individual blocks, particularly if cavalry are involved.

When the undercoat is thoroughly dry painting may commence. One would imagine that the application of paint is a comparatively simple matter, but judging by the number of articles that appear it would seem that the collector must surely have to have aspirations as a professional artist. Like so many things nowadays, the whole business has been enlarged out of all proportion and become esoteric.

The examination of a Britains' factory-painted hollow-cast shows that it fulfils certain obvious requirements. The paint is applied in the required places, the horse is brown or black or dappled, the face is one tone, with slight 'blushes' on the cheeks, and the eyes are indicated by a dot of black. The same principle applies to most other hollow-casts, and alkathene models, except that in the case of the latter the eyes are not indicated at all, nor are the 'blushes'. A model by Courtenay is basically the same, except that the quality of the paintwork and the colour is infinitely better, the application more exact, and attention to the horses far greater.

The characteristics of a Greenwood & Ball original, however, is that every area is outlined by the finest hairline of a darker colour. Ping and Brunoe have a restrained type of painting that is entirely their own, where no emphasis is placed on any one portion: only very occasionally do they allow themselves the luxury of a faintly indicated fold, or a slight change in colour on a silk coat, and Series 77, after initial errors in emphasis, have settled down to a fine, restrained style. Berdou's horses are perfect in their, what seems inevitable, display of skill and taste. Like Higgins, Stadden's own original painting went a small step further, with emphasis on the modelling, but still with care and restraint.

People obviously think of painting in different ways, but one factor must not be overlooked in any school of thought, and that is the size of the model involved. Logically, the largest should receive the boldest treatment, the smallest a more detailed approach, but in practice one sees results that falsify the argument. To revert to Britain's models, they gave what was wanted; to repaint them if battered seems a crime, as, indeed, it is with any older model. The only exception that might be made is in the case of the 'Knights of Agincourt' or the Timpo medieval sets, where, as the heraldic colours were only approximate, the models are enhanced by a more careful treatment. A higher class than the commercial painting is one in which painting is done with accuracy and taste, giving a fuller realisation of the importance of the hands and the face in bringing a model to life. This may be done in gloss, semi-gloss or matt paint, either in oils or in enamels, or a mixture of both. Eriksson's 40mm gems are painted in semi-gloss, the original Higgins miniatures in matt oils.

A further stage is reached when the paint is manipulated in such a way as to simulate every crease, every nuance of light and shade, every strand of hair, every darkening of flesh or hide, every contrasting edge of clothing or equipment, even down to the shading of the irises and the pupils of the eyes. (An example of the ultimate in painting is the complaint of one collector that the peak of a helmet on a 90mm model shaded the eye so that he had to recarve it before it could be painted. As there would already be a heavy shadow cast across the eyes from the peak it seems mere vanity to introduce detail which in life would not exist.)

It is at this stage, perhaps, that the collector might well pause and ask himself, 'what do I want of my model?' If he values the crispness and beauty of sculpture, when the *raison d'être* for this sculpture is to lend animation to an inanimate object, he might pause before he puts in that dark shadow in the fold of the sleeve and the highlight on the top edge; he may consider the size of the eye relative to the area of a face of a 54mm figure, let alone that of a 30mm flat; that an overlapping object is throwing its own necessary but inconspicuous shadow. If, having weighed up all these considerations, he decides that he does need all these things, he must then have the necessary skill to carry out this exacting task, and stand by the results. If he has not, it is far better for him to be honest and paint honestly, otherwise a highly wrought but unimaginative and possibly vulgar model may result. He need, of course, do neither, but send the model to one of the many studios that now undertake to paint any figure in professional style. Obviously it is advisable to ask for an estimate first.

Many of the studios employ artists of quite exceptional talent, and there are also the 'journeymen' whose job it is to animate or paint models for a maker either for display purposes or to satisfy purchasers. Again, many of these are men of excellent taste. However, it must be said that there are also a number of painters to whom dealers or agents pass their models, so that they may place the painted article on the shelves in their shops, and the quality of these is not so reliable. I remember very clearly a Series 77 nude Greek that was the abomination of the painted model. Here was a muscular figure, beautifully sculpted, the rib cages and muscles already very evident in the sculpture, made to appear as a vulgar athlete; pubic hair was emphasised, and contours heavily outlined with reddish ochre, so that the figure appeared to have received a thousand cuts, while the face was like that of some actor seen at close quarters with all the make-up of heavy-lidded oblong eyes, lined nose, and startling mouth. The whole effect was one of coarseness and bad taste, and perhaps it is best not to mention what has been done to those nubile nudes by Sanderson, Surén and Gammage!

On the other hand, the apogee is reached when everything blends miraculously into a harmonious whole, until one cannot tell where the modelling ends and the painting begins. The remarkable advance in the quality of colour photography of models, pioneered and promulgated so well by Philip Stearns, is a two-edged sword; any inherent weakness in painting, especially of facial expression, the shadows on the sides of the nose, the highlighting of the cheeks, the distortion of the eyes, is emphasised in reproduction, and becomes far more apparent than it does to the naked eye. One would do well, therefore, to consider this aspect when one reads two full pages of painting instructions, showing how to sit so that the light falls over the left shoulder (surely a thing known since the beginning of time), together with diagrams of a face and its contours, and an eye with its pupil and lashes; and does it really require a whole article to tell one how to paint a landschnecht, surely one of the easiest of models to paint, inasmuch as imagination in colour can be used to a far greater extent that with a French hussar or a Luftwaffe parachutist?

Conversely, a Peter Gilder can make a miracle of a 20mm figure, using a line so fine that one cannot conceive of a brush with so few hairs that it is still capable of lifting paint from a palette and placing it on a model; recently a breath-taking flat of the chariot of Senacherib was exhibited that matched the work of the continental professional painters of flats. The growing popularity of the polystyrene kit has been responsible for the evolution of a group of professional painters specialising in this type of model, and their skill both in conversion (for many do this as well) and in finish is such that when the model is completed it is impossible to tell that it is not made of lead. Names that spring to mind are those of Ray Lamb, Cèsar Milani-Gallieni, Pièrre Conrad and Lynn Sangster, whilst in the United States, Burke, Thompson, Fenerin, Stauffer, Berton, Todd and Scott, among many others, are kept amply employed.

The most traditional method of the use of oils is possibly the most satisfactory, even allowing for the slowness of drying. One of the ways in which a toy-like shine may be avoided is to mix the paint with turpentine rather than with a medium, and then when completely dry (up to a fortnight) paint over a light coat of clear varnish. The result is a compromise between a gloss and a matt surface. A great range of blending and subtle shading may be achieved by this method. It would be arrogant to lay down any fixed laws as to what range of colour should be used, or even attempt to enumerate the various tints needed for any specific part of the body. One might just as well attempt to dictate to a landscape painter the colours he should use. The only useful point would be to say that the fewer the basic colours the better. The modeller should be able to discover for himself which are the necessities and which are the ones to be used sparingly for specific details.

Those collectors, however, who prefer their figures to resemble as much as possible the actual material, may use a whole array of water, casein, or gouache-based colours, such as Humbrol matt enamel, Pelikan Plaka, Campaign Colours, or the ranges supplied by the British Model Soldier Society, Gammage, and Imrie-Risley. These have the advantage of drying much more quickly than oils, so that the completion of a model is speeded up. Shading, merging and blending may be done just as easily, and light colours superimposed upon or run across darker ones quite successfully. Specific hues and variations of khaki etc, are available in most of these ranges, thus eliminating colour mixing, and the various types may be used together. One would venture to suggest, however, that all figures painted in any type of matt finish should be treated with a thin coating of clear varnish, otherwise grease from fingers can easily appear on the surface. Flats are sometimes painted in this way, indeed water-colour is occasionally used, with a basic undercoat of gold size or even vinegar.

Each collector will discover for himself the method of working most appropriate to his own personality, whether he uses Humbrol enamels direct from the tins, or whether he transfers a quantity of each colour to a series of shallow dishes. Any attempts at painting, however, are governed by the brush, and every one of these should be of good quality (those issued by Historex have the advantage of very long bristles). It hardly seems necessary to have a brush consisting of a couple of hairs; and to apply paint from the end of a cocktail stick or sharpened match would perhaps seem to indicate that the painter is trying to achieve too much. Nor can it be said that the use of a magnifying glass is necessary, even in the most delicate work. This would indicate that the finished model itself would have to be viewed through the same glass, an unnecessary procedure. (Many of the models illustrated in this book were painted by the author. The only brushes used were of 0, 1, and 2 size.)

It would appear logical to paint the large areas of the model first, such as the jackets and trousers, completing them before proceeding to smaller details, but a number of collectors prefer to paint the flesh parts first as a key to the whole colour scheme. The advantage appears to be that if, for example, one has a model whose face should be, by the action of the model, choleric, the brighter tones of the cheeks and the general expression of rage should be highlighted by the surrounding colours. On the other hand, a contemplative face might be enhanced by a softening of the adjacent areas. Valentine Bean, a collector of flats, wrote two most interesting articles on the painting of these, selecting as his theme two allied subjects Neckel's 'The Trophies of Austerlitz', and Scholz's 'The Burning of the Standards.' In the first the emphasis was on activity, light, colour, triumph: in the second, the sombreness of defeat. The sets were painted accordingly, so that each expressed a different emotion.

With flats is is essential to convey the impression of a three-dimensional object, so that a rider, for example, is actually sitting on his horse and is not an extension of it. This can, one feels, be done quite boldly, using a single firm line rather than a multitude of tiny ones, and wargame models might well be treated in the same way.

The largest areas having been completed, detail may now be attempted. Where a narrow emphatic line is required, it can sometimes be helpful to paint a strip of the darker colour around the required area, and the contrasting colour superimposed until the hair's breadth line is left untouched rather than paint in the line itself. Metals can be simulated by leaving the portion of the casting unpainted, and polishing with a burnisher, or by the use of the various types of gold, silver, bronze and gun-metal paint available (of which Winsor & Newton's Florentine Liquid Leaf is very popular). Gold shows up best if painted over a dark ground. Gun-metal is useful for the duller parts of armour, such as chain-mail.

Alkathene models should, for permanence, be undercoated, although many collectors do not consider this necessary. With polystyrene, however, no undercoat is needed, but much more care has to be taken with the quality of the paint used, and whichever type is preferred, it must be applied very thinly. At first, there may be disappointment with the result, and only constant practice will overcome a tendency for a mottled effect to result, especially on large areas. Much advice has been given very often on how to paint horses, and to add to this would only cause greater confusion. As with so many other activities, one has to discover one's own way over difficulties.

Page 143 (*above*) A group of unusual models: back row: plaster, by Hahn; mounted chessman by Mokarex; 54mm lead Russian cavalryman, moulded on one side only, by Peter David; mounted chessman by Stadden. Front row: typical crude modern continental semi-solid; pressed-out metal colour-printed Nazi cigarette card; 'fun figure' in turned wood; German cut-out cardboard; late nineteenth-century semi-flat; modern continental semi-flat in pewter; 'sardine-tin' figure printed in colour, with flanged footstand; (*below*) Commemorative: Major General F. Williams, 'the Hero of Kars', 1855. A large plaster model, typical of that period.

Page 144 Contemporary: large (230mm) equestrian model of a captain of the 9th Hussars, France, c1810, made in fibreglass resin by Pierre Turner. Peter Wilcox is an amateur modeller of outstanding ability and imagination. This model of a Varangian guardsman, on which a number of techniques are used, won the Medieval Trophy at the British Model Soldier Society competition in 1970.

In discussing painting it has so far been assumed that the model is an assembled one. However, one well known exhibitor and writer admits that his eyesight and the unsteadiness of his hand are not equal to this, and many models are indeed issued in kit form. The main bulk of the figure presents no new problems, once as many parts as possible have been assembled, but many of the additional pieces are of awkward shape and may be difficult to paint on the otherwise completed model. The problem is in holding the piece in such a way as to be able to completely cover it in paint, and yet not smear or remove the colour in handling. The only suggestion that can be made is to place the object flat on a working surface, and apply the paint to whatever portions one can see. When dry, it can then be placed at another angle, or turned over, and the process repeated. Most difficult of all are the minutiae of buttons, badges, cords and the like, as used in polystyrene kits, and it is better to paint these whilst they are still on the sprue. The lightest touch of adhesive will subsequently have to be used. One of the disadvantages of painting every piece separately before assembly is that one has to be very sure that the adhesive will not ooze out and discolour the paint. Segom, in fact, issue a warning that any type of paint on one of their models acts as an insulator, and, consequently, as acetone is a paint solvent, any separately painted parts will not hold together when adhesive is applied. Therefore, the model has to be painted as a whole.

Perhaps the ultimate in painting is reached by the use of an airbrush on the horse of a 54mm model. For a manufacturer with a large output one imagines that the saving of time and hand-labour might well warrant the cost of £30 or £40, but for a collector to purchase one is probably a slight extravagance.

13

COLLECTING AND DISPLAY

A number of methods of collecting soldiers are possible, or no method at all. The best is that which gives the greatest pleasure to the collector. The most obvious is the non-method of accumulation, which probably occurs at one time or other to most of us. One may begin with the purchase of a set, perhaps in plastic, of one period; this is followed by another, equally attractive, of a different era; one's attention is then taken by something entirely different. Wargame models begin to fill the drawers of cabinets, flats sprout from cupboards, boxes of unpainted castings litter the attic. Napoleonic grenadiers jostle medieval knights; Nazi storm-troopers and Afrika Korps stand cheek by jowl with Greeks and Romans; British line regiments tread on the toes of Cromwellians. Scattered amongst this motley throng shy and timid women, perhaps partly nude, peer nervously across at ravening Huns. There may be a special corner devoted to artillery, armoured vehicles and the like, or a wargame table may dominate the room, or half-dissected Historex and Airfix kits litter the sideboard.

After the first rosy flush of acquisition (which may last many years) a collector may begin to tire of this hugger-mugger, and decide to weed his collection (and how many have later had cause to regret it!). What is to be weeded is decided by what course of action he hopes to take in the future.

The hobby as a whole may be based on three primary groups:

1 Round models (hollow-casts, solids, plastics, irrespective of size or make)
2 Flats
3 Rounds and flats

Added to these are three ancillary groups of recent growth, whose activities are not primarily based on the accepted convention of collecting:

A The wargamer
B The acquirer of polystyrene kits solely as a vehicle for alteration
C The purchaser of armoured fighting vehicles, usually for a similar purpose, and to whom the presence of figures is of secondary account

Within each of these categories there are two prime considerations of which the first is finance. It is useless to attempt the acquisition of a collection of the highest quality unless one can afford the models of such makers as Berdou and des Fontaines, as the price will, over the years, be prohibitive. To commence the collecting of Courtenays at their present price (and one cannot see a diminution of this) also calls for serious thought, as does the seeking out of the rarer Britains items.

Secondly, and of equal importance, available space must be considered. If a large room can be devoted to the display of models little difficulty arises, but even so it may surprise many a budding collector to find how readily all his space may be filled to overflowing. Should there be only a limited display area, frustration may well be experienced when the boxes and the plastic envelopes and the mini-dioramas have to be consigned to the roof of the garage or the loft. After all, no collector works in a vacuum, and one of the joys of collecting is the sharing with others of one's particular range of interests. The space needed for conversion of models is by no means negligible; on the other hand, only a relatively small area is necessary for painting, and this should present few problems.

Bearing these factors in mind, let us look at the principal facet of the model-soldier world, rounds. Within this orbit there is hardly a limit. Examination of a number of collections reveals some basic themes:

1 The embracing of all makers of all periods and styles irrespective of whether the models are in metal or other materials. This will include specimens from many countries, and many periods will figure; there will be toys and there will be masterpieces.

2 Britains, and/or those manufacturers who deliberately copied or pirated their models.

3 Britains and commercial manufacturers both in hollow-cast and other materials, such as Timpo, Heyde, Mignot, Authenticast, S.A.E. and Elastolin.

4 Makers of solids of better quality, such as Stadden, Greenwood & Ball, Gammage, Hinton, and the more recent British, American and continental makers.

5 The medievalists, with Courtenay and Ping as a basis.

6 Alkathene only.

7 The finest quality only, irrespective of maker.

These types of collections may again be broken down, revealing a preponderance of one period, perhaps the Ancient World, or the Middle Ages, the sixteenth to eighteenth centuries, the years of massed nations in conflict, the American Revolution, the American Civil War, the Crimean War, the British Colonial Wars, the lull before the storm, World Wars I and II. In these instances the collector will endeavour to acquire representative models by as many makers and in as many different styles, sizes and materials as he is able within his special period.

These sub-divisions are again capable of dissection, and whilst one collector will concentrate on French troops of the First Empire, another will collect the British and Allied troops of the same period, and yet another the Russians. One collector is known to fit his medieval models, whether metal, or plastic, *au naturel* or converted, into a vast unfinished reconstruction of Poitiers; another occupies himself solely with artillery officers through the ages. British regimental bands are the concern of a number of collectors, whilst others concentrate on the development of uniform of a specific unit, or group of units.

The collectors of flats are a dedicated race, guided over the years by the Bantocks, who search eagerly the lists of the continental makers and distributors, and make the annual pilgrimage to Kulmbach. Their range of interests follow closely on those of the collectors of the larger models: either an all-embracing scope, or 'type' examples, or a concentration on either period, style or engraver. They have the advantage in that their models are nearly all within the same narrow range of size, they are easily stored, and are relatively far less expensive.

The wargamers, as has been seen, employ their models for a set purpose, and there can be few purchasers of a Historex assembly who purchase it for its own sake. One feels that the same applies to the armoured fighting vehicle fraternity: their models are used for purpose rather than display.

The classical form of collecting is the acquisition of a model as an entity in itself: nothing else is required of it than it should satisfy its owner. To exhibit its virtues to the best advantage it should be mounted on a small pedestal. A model up to 60mm is quite adequately served by a block $\frac{3}{4}$in tall, with a chamfered-edged top large enough to accommodate the footstand, which is normally 1 to $1\frac{1}{2}$sq in, although some action models require a greater length than breadth, whilst, of course, mounted models take up a proportionately large area. For such items as an artillery team an increase in the height of the block should be made. The colour is a matter of preference, but generally speaking a medium or reddish mahogany seems ideal. However, the issuing of moulded black polystyrene bases is now quite common, and there is today far more opportunity for a mixture of materials and shapes. I have at times actually used obtuse-angled white-plastic stands, or even plasticised matchbox covers, subsequently coated with gold paint, especially for rococo subjects. Whatever the surface, it is surprising how the slight extra height lends dignity to even a humble model.

Larger models require taller pedestals, and much use may be made of socles such as those given with miniature trophies (Higgins used these with his 54mm samples, but they seem slightly overpowering at this size). Smaller models, say 30mm downwards, should not be scaled down, and the same height of block seems quite proper. Ideally, the smaller the model the more necessary it is to combine several figures on one stand – the models of Eriksson, Surén, Stadden and Lamming are ideally suited to this purpose. The really tiny ones, again, might well be grouped, although an experiment with a single model on a varnished cotton reel sometimes gives surprising results.

The majority of the French makers of the finest models screw a gilded name plate to the front of the stand, upon which the legend is carefully engraved, and this certainly gives the model an added dignity. Many collectors do this by means of hand lettering rather than engraving, but one has to be expert in this art. For those who do not wish to undertake this task there are several lettering machines on the market.

It was the practice of older collectors to paint the footstand of the model (if not already done) and then affix it directly on to the top of the wood plinth. The more modern concept is to create a little more atmosphere by using a ground in keeping with the model. A South African war infantryman could, for example, stand upon a sandy patch, a British tommy in simulated mud, a Cossack in deep snow, or an eighteenth-century grandee on a flagged pavement. The fact that most fighting occurs in the open presupposes the extensive use of green to represent grass, but there are many shades of the colour. An effective impression is obtained by building up a very thin layer of Polyfilla or similar substance on the top of the base and pressing the figure gently into it. Excess plaster should be immediately removed. When the mixture is set the top can be coated with glue and flock grass of various colours sprinkled upon it. When it is dry the residue can be removed by dusting or brushing, and any portions which have not adhered given a second application. The type of material used by the model railway enthusiasts is ideal, and finely sieved sand can be used in the same way. If required, a stronger impression may be obtained by the use of simulated grass or actual pebbles, but these should be left to the larger groups, except in the case of a pair of contestants or a dismounted cavalryman leading his horse, and similar compositions.

When several models are incorporated on the same stand, care should be taken with proportions: the top of the surface should not be so large that the models become too isolated, nor so small that they are crowded. There is now no limit to the ingenuity that may be displayed, although many collectors prefer little or no scenery. The only constant factor is a plaster base, and good taste. Pebbles, actual sand, placticine, glass, pieces of mirror, cellophane, actual twigs, pieces of equipment, grass made from teased sisal, commercial moss, pieces of discarded armour, weapons, broken gun-wheels and the like may all be pressed into service. The one thing that should be carefully considered is the overall effect: a scene of jubilation calls for strong colour, of desolation or defeat sombreness. Even so there is a risk of overdoing brilliancy; at an exhibition in London recently a beautifully arranged and painted combat group of Surén's finest 40mm knights was ruined for me by the excessive length of the grass, and its pre-Raphaelite intense green clashed heavily with the blazonry on the figures.

Balance between models is needed, as well as composition, neither of which can be taught. Perhaps the ideal conception is for the 'conversation-piece' of two or three models in 54mm scale, with an overall size for the top of the stand of from 6 to 9in. It is effective on occasions to make the terrain of an irregular shape rather than take it to the extreme limit of the stand – this is very effective in the display of a unified group of wargame figures.

It should be emphasised that these assemblies or 'mini-dioramas' are without backgrounds and intended for viewing from any angle. From there it is a logical step to the full diorama, and it is here, above all, that the flat comes into its own. One has only to study one of the classic examples, such as the 'Crecy' or 'Plassey' formerly at the Royal United Service Institution to understand one of the prime reasons for flats. They can be used in thousands, as is general on the Continent, or in the smallest of groups. The area they occupy is governed by the reason for their assembly and the function they are designed to fulfil. Denny Stokes, who in the 1940s had so much to do with the development of the diorama in England, could present a perfect Napoleon surveying the coast of Britain from France, in a box a foot long, using six flats; the great 'Siege of Vienna' made by a team of Austrian collectors utilises some thousands. There are, however, one or two pitfalls that should be avoided, and into which even the professionals occasionally fall. One is to decide the position of the sun before painting the models otherwise shadows will be thrown in different directions. Similarly, the direction from which the wind (if any) is to blow should be noted. One classic example, a fine diorama of the Battle of Morat, has two sets of banners and standards within a few inches of each other which are blowing stiffly in opposite directions.

The makers of dioramas and the wargamers alike can call upon many modern aids unheard of some ten years ago. The essential for each is a firm foundation upon which to build their effects. There are, of course, basic initial differences; the dioramist will enclose his finished product in a glass-fronted box, whereas the wargamer may well dismantle his terrain. In the first the footstands of the models have to be concealed, in the second the models will most probably be left mounted in batches on a common base. The dioramist will need a painted backcloth, whilst the wargamer's table will be open to view from all sides.

The actual construction of a base must depend on size and shape. Basically, if contours are needed, they may be made from layers decreasing in size of polystyrene tiles, wood blocks, rolled paper and the like, covered with fine-mesh wire or linen over which plaster is applied, and the models sunk into it. Rivers and roads, ruts, and other natural features may be applied or carved out of the plaster. Hedges, trees and bushes are obtainable in appropriate sizes, together with fences and stone walls. Gun emplacements, gabions, trenches, redoubts and the like are also on the market, together with bridges of all kinds, period houses and farms (from the Jew's House at Lincoln to Neufwanstein Castle, from a farmhouse to Hougoumont, from a country church to Ulm Cathedral) in plastic or card, painted or unpainted, together with Roman forts and medieval strongholds, even in 5mm size. Gone are the days of the cardboard shoebox and the sheets of printed paper bricks and tiling. Any building not readily available may be carved from the incredible polystyrene square. And even interiors are available, together with period furnishings and fittings. As a background, there is nothing really to equal a well-designed and painted original. Either the collector can draw or he cannot – it is as simple as that. If he is not sufficiently proficient, he will have to use an enlarged photograph.

Any model exposed to air collects dust, which is difficult to remove from folds and crevices. It is wise therefore to house them behind glass. All types of display cases and cabinets are available from bookcases to those used for the display of china. The ideal for a normal collection is one that fits on a wall with sliding glass doors without glazing bars and glass shelves. The models gain an added stature and interest by illuminating them with small fluorescent lighting tubes, which are, of course, a necessity in a diorama. For a 'mini-diorama' or the larger model a glass or good quality plastic cover or dome is essential.

Flats can be well displayed in narrow, shallow shelves: a hanging case made from a large picture frame is ideal. For storage or exhibition they can be kept in flat boxes similar to those used by photographic suppliers for large sheets of negative paper. Into the lower portion of the box a sheet of thin polystyrene tiling may be inserted, and slots cut in the surface in which one half of the footstand rests; or a stout piece of black card shaped into a tray, making an admirable foil for the display of colour. The size of the box will of course depend on the number of individual items there are in the set to be displayed.

With the growth of the hobby, and the interest that it has aroused in many non-military or non-collecting circles there has been an enormous increase in the number of exhibitions of parochial and national and international level, and one of the first things a collector may wish to do is to become a member of a society. The British Model Soldier Society has been in being since 1935, and its membership has increased vastly over the years. Its meetings are normally held in London, but there is a nation-wide coverage formed by offshoots and divisions from the main stem, so that members can equally well attend meetings in the North, the Midlands, the South East, the South West, and East Anglia. There is ample opportunity for the display of one's own models, whether painted castings, conversions, original conceptions or collector's pieces, and competitions are held with regularity.

This is the pattern set for most other societies, and there are many such in practically every country or continent. It is at the meetings of these societies that a collector may well display a model that attracts so much attention that he may decide to become a professional, and it is through their journals that news of new models, articles on old ones, and information regarding uniform and military history in general may be gleaned. The wargamers and the converters also have their own special societies, and here again many more branches open regularly in various parts of any country that one likes to mention.

There is a large and steadily growing body of collectors whose interest lies in the non-military direction and who are as keen on the acquisition of the model of a farmer or a ballerina or a famous actress, either to exhibit them in their own right, or to incorporate them with their models of fighting men. There is a greater need for models of people of all ages than the average manufacturer realises, and the corpus of what has been produced merely touches the surface of what might be done. A few enlightened makers appreciated this early on, especially in Central Europe, where the tin manufacturers, who had begun with objects of a religious significance, then turned to military ones, but seriously challenged the popularity of the latter by making delightful, if naïve, sets of peasants, market fairs, townsfolk, railway scenes, mountaineering parties, rococo gardens and pavilions, carriages, hunts, dances, circus performers, and the like.

Heinrichsen, among the welter of military figures, produced a medieval market, complete with running pigs and chasing children, and his tournament set contains spectators and jesters. In our own time Hafer has produced many sets of ancient, mythological and medieval subjects, whilst Rössner is noted for his peasants, fairy stories and portrait models, and Scholtz has many delightful civilians in his vast output. Opera, the stage, and Wagnerian saga has also been portrayed by various makers.

Royalty has an obvious attraction, and it was his 'Coronation' group that brought Gammage to the fore. Gottstein designed a set of flats of English kings and queens, which were cast and marketed by Carman. Almirall has a set of those of Spain: Mokarex and Mignot have produced a number of French ones, and Café Storme the whole gamut of Belgian. The nearest approach we have in England is a long series, every model different, that Ping has been making for his clients over the years, especially of the House of Plantagenet. Courtenay made a few, including Charles II in two versions, George V and Queen Mary. Henry VIII and Elizabeth I have always been popular, and the Coronation of Elizabeth II brought forth models by a number of makers. Frontier is commencing what one would like to hope will be a definitive set upon its completion.

Individual monarchs have been produced by many makers in all countries and in all media, together with the ladies and gentlemen of the court, but not in any regular series. Vertunni was the most prolific, making perhaps 350 lovely models (in solid or hollow-cast) of royalty and important personages in history: some of these are predictable, such as Joan of Arc and Napoleon, but many civilians are included. They are now extremely rare and much sought after for their artistry. There are so many famous people throughout history the list is endless, and yet so few have been commemorated.

Ordinary folk, also, going about their daily tasks, can be just as fascinating as their military counterparts, as evinced by the two series, each quite remarkable in themselves, but quite different, the one of ancient peoples, mainly Egyptian, who complement Gammage's gods and goddesses, and the Roman slave market by Sanderson. Brunoe's females are full of grace and attractiveness, and form ideal counterparts to their galant partners. Alymer's series of ancient warlike races are so attractive that perhaps ordinary people will be added to them. One occasionally comes across a stray medieval lady in plastic from some obscure maker, but the most attractive are the 40mm Berliner specimens, complete with children, and including one or two equestrienne hawking models, and the lovely Starlux figures. There are a few females of the succeeding centuries (Surén, Higgins, Ping, Brunoe, Hinton, Stadden) but generally speaking for representations of contemporary types we have to look to the makers of hollow-casts and plastics, where there is a varied assortment of people engaged in trade, sport, and occasionally, religious activity (Britains' Salvation Army, S.A.E.'s Papal choir). Britains, Timpo, Hill, Cherilea, Charbens, Benbros and the like made almost as many non-military as military models, many of them setting problems for collectors as to 'date' and 'issue'. As far as attractiveness is concerned, it would be hard to beat the Britains–Herald plastic models, especially those of the farmer, his wife and the landgirl, and their 'school of riding' set; whilst they are right up to date with motorcycle and moped teenagers.

These civilian models make a very attractive display in any collection either when grouped together or when an individual model is added to a military one, an aspect occasionally favoured by the professional maker.

Weapons of all ages have been produced by practically every maker, and a separate section might well be formed by the collector. Those of ancient and medieval times have always been favoured by makers, and Hinchliffe, Lamming, Laing and others have many such among the 'tinies', with Britains, Lone Star, Crescent and Elastolin in the larger sizes. The latter, in particular, has a remarkable siege tower in two sizes, and Mertens do scaling-ladders and other ancillaries such as mantlets. Elastolin also features a fine Renaissance cannon with a suitably armed crew. The makers of flats have provided suitable artillery for every age (many incorporating men and weapon on one stand) and the artillery of the Napoleonic age has been a favourite with most designers of solids and plastics, both large and small (Dickinson, Heroics 5mm; Laing 15mm; Hinchliffe 20, 25, 54mm; Douglas, Airfix 20mm; Lamming, Phoenix 25mm; Warrior 30mm; Imrie–Risley, Almirall, Alcocer, Britains, Historex, Gammage, Mignot 54mm).

Britains made many late nineteenth- and early twentieth-century cannon, some now very rare, and the Colonial wars are fairly well served. Artillery of World War I and II proliferate (Britains, Almark, Hinchliffe, Elastolin, Tamiya, Imrie–Risley and many others): indeed, it would be an impossible task to list them all. Many, but not all, are supplied with the necessary teams of horses and men and the ammunition wagons. Some of the larger and more involved pieces are miracles of construction, especially those in polystyrene, and may well need the efforts of a team rather than of an individual to assemble them. The tiny ones, also, are equally intricate. This is of course, a highly specialised study in itself, but by and large the makers appear to satisfy their clients, and far less amendment seems to be necessary with the hyper-critical than is the case with the actual men themselves.

Collectors with limited space may well be attracted by the smaller units, such as the Britains naval cannon and crew, the Imrie–Risley Burgundian bombard and gunner, the gun-deck of an eighteenth-century privateer, the 9-pounder naval gun and sailor, and the 32-pounder carronade and officer of 1812.

The study of military uniform and equipment has become a latterday religion in collecting circles, and there has never been such a proliferation of 'militaria' societies. Everyman has now become his own historian and critic, and woe betide the designer who makes an error. Hardly a model is produced that is not subjected to the most rigorous examination by the reviewer and the collector. It is not sufficient for the maker to have had a long and honourable career, for there is always someone with that little extra specialised knowledge who, in the name of course, of accuracy, will attempt to pull him down from his eminent position.

Today's emphasis is on accuracy of uniform and anatomy; little allowance or patience is displayed for the maker who seeks to break away from the strictly authentic but deadly dull model by exercising his imagination either in conception or in treatment. One sees, for example, a 30mm war-elephant criticised in a review as being 'too fanciful' (why not?); an otherwise 'splendid horse' has a tail that the critic would prefer to be 'hanging down close to the buttocks', and 'only a little work is required on the girth and the bit'; a French voltiguer officer needs his hair 're-texturing, and the embroidered horns on his turnback require replacement with the Historex ones.' A very large model, intended by the designer as a statuette, and admitted by the reviewer to be of high decorative quality, is then condemned for its elegant pose (or perhaps for its imaginative qualities?), and the crowning indignity is reached when it is suggested that a 'bit of dirt under the fingernails would add realism'.

This all seems very frivolous, when compared with the suggestions about the same model that the gun is over-long, the sword too short, the pouches and epaulettes the wrong shape, the slashes of the cuffs rectangular instead of three-pointed, the turnbacks too large, and that the pack has to be completely re-worked, and fresh belts and buckles supplied. Of an Airfix trooper of the 10th Regiment of Hussars it is stated that his trews are 'light tan and in fact the inner leg and bottom edges should be tan or light brown and they had a thin leather trim for grip. These are shown with a yellow stripe and his barrel sash is red and yellow.' (An interesting exchange of views took place following these statements, covering several weeks and by different correspondents.)

Of the sabre of an American 54mm model it was said that 'the hilt had to be completely carved out,' and 'spurs had to be made from fuse wire'; of the Airfix Scots Greys 'there should be a buckle slide and tip in brass on the pouch crossbelt and there should be only two rings on the sabretache ... the carbine should be the 1800 pattern Paget ... the clip on the sling goes directly on to (the slide) not as shown, with a leather strap.'

Nor was this the end. 'The plume should be white over red: the bearskin is black with a red patch on top bearing the white horse of Hanover badge ... at the front was a brass badge of the Royal Arms below which was a black leather peak.' This criticism brought the response: 'the bearskin did not have a red patch ... and the brass plate displayed a thistle surrounded by a circlet bearing the motto *Nemo Me Impure Lacessit*; the plume was white, framing the red which was superimposed ... the tails of the horses were long after 1764 (not short as in the kit).' Another expert then joined in with: 'the Scots Greys wore an all-white plume throughout their history, scarlet plumes being worn only by the musicians and trumpeters.' Perhaps the last word was said when another historian, quoting from seven standard reference works, said that the white plume has a red cloth patch at the rear, and that the designer of the original model was right after all.

It may be thought that overmuch emphasis has been placed on what must be a commonplace of present-day collecting, but it demonstrates the importance placed on accuracy above all other considerations. (Ray Lamb took a whole year to research his 6in Saburai.) At the same time it shows how divergent are the views of writers and collectors on their own chosen subject. One may legitimately suggest that a model is clumsy in its stance, that the details are badly sculptured, or that the horses are lacking in movement – these remarks are based on experience and sensitivity, but criticism of uniform or equipment must be backed by the most intensive knowledge of military history. It is in this department that doubts are being expressed as to the competency of many present-day collectors and others who write about models. One critic, for example, goes so far as to suggest that the only authorities upon whom one could rely are the continentals and W. Y. Carman, the brothers Mollo, and the late René North. This may appear to some as an extreme statement, but it is worth mentioning that it was revealed recently after lengthy charge and counter-charge that a reviewer of 20mm military models for a certain illustrated monthly journal, was forced to admit that not only had he never heard of the eminent designer, but that he knew nothing at all about model soldiers, his interests being fighting vehicles! Furthermore, a warning was given recently by a reader that the information given in the same journal by some of the correspondents should be viewed with caution, unverified as it was by the editorial staff.

It has been pointed out that one of the difficulties of laying down hard and fast rules about uniforms is that basically there never were any until possibly the 1900 dress regulations were brought in. Prior to this there were many variations, especially for short periods and often by very small units, thus making an exhaustive and comprehensive study the occupation of a lifetime. All references to uniform and equipment, therefore, should be treated with caution, but at the same time it would be stupid to allow a minor discrepancy to interfere with ones enjoyment of the hobby.

Sources of information are, of course, many and varied, indeed, at times they appear almost too prolific, and to acquire a complete library of all the published material of the last few years, to say nothing of the masterpieces of the past, would be a highly expensive business.

A number of makers include either painting instructions or a coloured illustration (sometimes both) with their models, some extremely detailed, others again mere sketchy introductions. Magazines, mainly catering for converters and armoured fighting vehicle enthusiasts, at the same time devote a proportion of their space to a review of current models, and publish articles on uniforms, as for example a long series in *Military Modelling* by Dino Lemonofides on the colours of the British army.

The best of these journals is undoubtedly *Tradition*, published by Norman Newton Ltd, which contains in each issue an amazing amount of information of the most varied kind. To take an issue at random: Recollections of a Prussian Hussar; the Wargame; Prussian Dragoons (1740–86); German Assault Troops (1914–18); British and French Infantry in the Peninsula; The Bikanir Camel Corps (1897); Armoured Trains in Egypt (1882), accompanied by colour plates and line drawings. Regimental house magazines are also a most valuable source of information, as are also the volumes of *The Navy and Army Illustrated*, even though the plates are not coloured.

Regimental museums themselves may help with the solution of knotty problems, although here again a certain amount of conjecture as far as colour is concerned may arise, because the production methods that existed could vary considerably in the dyes, resulting in a discrepancy in colours. On the other hand, a visit may be rewarding, as curators are often eager to help with a problem, and some, indeed, have been known to go to immense personal trouble to arrive at a solution.

The most usual approach by the collector is for him to refer to a book or series of books relating to his particular interest, and there are today many such available. Here again, a warning may not come amiss, as some publications of recent years are not the result of original research, but put together hurriedly (possibly at the urgent request of a publisher) and relying mainly on their attractive appearance and low price. As the late René North has so rightly said 'many instances occur where authorities disagree on matters of detail, and where regulation dress was never worn, or again where the dress as worn was never authorized'.

To review the out-of-print, rarely accessible, and costly books on military costume, mainly of continental origin, would be tedious and unrewarding, but for the die-hard collector the auction catalogues of Sothebys, Christies, Sotheby-Parke Bernet, and Hauswedel and the lists and catalogues issued by antiquarian booksellers should be studied, although the prices will prove beyond the means of the average collector. There should be no difficulty, however, in finding new publications, for not only are they stocked by the majority of model shops, but advertisements and reviews appear regularly in trade and society journals. Such series as those issued by the Blandford Press, by Almark, Osprey and Castermann are so well known as not to merit further introduction. Less well known are sets of postcards and uniform sheets, mainly published on the Continent or at least promoted by French and German publications. There are welcome signs, however, that English publishers are making efforts to supplement these.

Finally, a scrapbook is a necessity. Nothing is more infuriating than to have remembered a reference illustration that has 'got away'. Better still is a logical system of filing cards, arranged according to the collector's requirements.

Even with a whole library of books on uniform and equipment, however, no serious collector will embark on making, painting or converting a model without being conversant with other factors such as the average height of a Celt as compared with a Gaul, the degree of curvature of the legs of a Scythian horse-archer as opposed to those of a Chinese bowman of the same period. Physiognomical characteristics, hair styles, both head and facial, the length of arms and legs, the colour of the skin of the various races, the slant of the eyes: all these anthropological details are important, as Peter Wilcox has graphically demonstrated.

The collector is thus well endowed with aids – it is now up to him as to how he uses them. The fascination of the model soldier hangs on two factors – either absolutely authentic detail in every possible respect, with the possibility of a resultantly lifeless figure, or an appreciation of reticence, with imagination creating the model that stands out from its fellows.

APPENDIX 1

Books for further reading

Where the place of publication is not given, it may be assumed that this is London.

Baldet, Marcel. *Figurines et Soldats de Plomb* (Paris, 1961)
Bard, Robert. *Making and Collecting Military Miniatures* (New York, 1957)
Blum, Peter. *Military Miniatures* (New York, 1964)
——. *The Model Soldier Manual* (New York, 1970)
Carman, W. Y. *Model Soldiers* (1973)
Clarétie, (L.) *Les Jouets: Histoire, Fabrication* (Paris, 1894)
Daiken L. *Children's Toys through the Ages* (1953)
——. *The World of Toys* (1963)
D'Allemagne, H. R. *Histoire des Jouets* (Paris, 1903)
Dilly, Maj. R. *Scale-model Soldiers* (1972)
Featherstone, Donald F. *Battles with Model Soldiers* (1972)
——. *Handbook for Model Soldier Collectors* (1969)
——. *Military Modelling* (1970)
Flick, Pauline. *Discovering Toys and Toy Museums* (1971)
Forrer, R. *Les Étains de la Collection Alfred Ritleng* (Strasbourg, 1905)
Fraser, Lady Antonia. *A History of Toys* (1966)
Freeman, R. and L. *Cavalcade of Toys* (New York, 1952)
Garratt, John G. *Model Soldiers: A Collector's Guide* (3rd ed 1971)
——. *Model Soldiers for the Connoisseur* (London and New York, 1973)
Grant, Charles. *The War Game* (1972)
Gripenberg Ole. *Tennsoldater* (Helsinki, 1973)
Hampe, T. *Der Zinnsoldat* (Berlin, 1924)
Harris, Maj. Henry. *How to Go Collecting Model Soldiers* (1969)
——. *Model Soldiers* (1962)
Hert, Louis. *Handbook of Old American Toys* (New York, 1947)
Holme, C. G., Ed. *Children's Toys of Yesterday* (1932)
Jackson, Mrs Neville. *Children's Toys of Other Days* (1908)

McClintock, Inez and Marshall. *Toys in America* (Washington, 1961)
Martin, Paul. *Les Petits Soldats de Strasbourg* (Strasbourg, 1950)
——. *Der Standhafte Zinnsoldat* (Berlin, 1962)
Martin, Paul and Vaillant, M. *Le Monde Merveilleux des Soldats de Plomb* (Paris, 1959)
Model Soldiers – Armies in Miniature, Introduction by Massimo Alberini (Novaro, 1972)
Nicholson, Lt-Col J. B. R. *Model Soldiers*, for Norman Newton Ltd (1969)
Nicollier, J. *Collecting Toy Soldiers* (Fribourg, 1967)
Ortmann, Erwin. *Zinnfiguren Einst und Jetzt* (Leipzig, 1972)
Percout, R. *Les Images d'Épinal* (Paris, 1912)
Richards, L. W. *Old British Model Soldiers*, 1893–1918 (1969)
Riff, A. *Les Étains Strasbourgeois du XVIe au XIXe Siècle* (Strasbourg, 1925)
Risley, C. A. and Imrie, W. F. *The Model Soldier Guide* (New York, 1967)
Scrine, J. *A Short History of Britains Ltd* (1955)
Taylor, Arthur. *Discovering Model Soldiers* (1970)
Teague, Dennis. *Discovering Modelling for Wargamers* (1973)
Tinge-linge-later, tinsoldater . . . (Copenhagen, 1966)

PERIODICALS

Airfix Magazine (PSL Publications Ltd, 9 Ely Place, London EC1) deals mainly with AFVs and aeroplanes, but there is an occasional mention of an Airfix model or a conversion.

Military Modelling (PO Box 35, Bridge Street, Hemel Hempstead, Herts.). Lavishly illustrated, many plates in colour, articles mainly on uniforms, A.F.Vs and conversions, but useful for reviews and advertisements of models.

Miniature Warfare and Model Soldiers (Stanhope House, Fairbridge Road, London N19) was the first general magazine in the field.

Modellismo Militaire (Casella Postale 1445, Firenze, Italy) is a new venture (1973) dealing more particularly with Italian models.

Tradition (Norman Newton Ltd, 188 Piccadilly, London W1) is outstanding in this field.

In all the above the many advertisements by dealers and agents and the notification of new models form a very useful guide for the serious collector.

APPENDIX 2

Dealers and agents

The following can only be regarded as a representative listing of the vast number of hobby stores that are to be found in most towns. It must be understood that stocks are subject to change. Where Greenwood & Ball is mentioned, their whole range (Greenwood & Ball, Garrison, Olive, Minot, Sanderson, Lasset) is to be understood.

CANADA

Derreck Miniatures, 96 Briscoe Street East, London, Ontario. (Almirall, Cavalier, Historex, Imrie–Risley, Little Generals, Monarch, Vallance)

R. Payen, Figurines Historiques, Box 62, Iberville, Quebec. (Almirall, Gammage, Historex, Old Guard, Segom, Surén)

DENMARK

Model og Hobby, Frederiksborg-gade 23, Copenhagen, K. (Almirall, Alymer, Brigader, Brunoe, Eriksson, Franke, Gammage, Garrison, Hinton, Historex H–R, Imrie–Risley, Krunert, Maier, Olive, Sentry Box, Sivhed, Surén, Trips, old Authenticast, Mokarex)

GREAT BRITAIN

The Armoury, 1 Fisher Road, Stoke, Plymouth, Devon. (Cavalier, Douglas, Gammage, Greenwood & Ball, Helmet, Hinchliffe, Hinton, Historex, Jac, Jackboot, Kirk, Lamming, Miniature Figurines, Phoenix, Segom, Stadden, Surén, Trophy)

E. Berwick, 11a, Newland Street, Kettering, Northants. (Douglas, Skybird)

Bridle Models, 2 Bridle Parade, Bridle Road, Shirley, Croydon, Surrey. (Historex, Minot, Phoenix, Series 77, Stadden)

Colberre Ltd, 48 Station Road, West Drayton, Middlesex. (Greenwood & Ball, Hinchliffe)

G. M. Haley, 5 Park Noon, Southowram, Halifax. (Mail-order – old Britains and their rivals and contemporaries)

Hamleys, Regent Street, London, W1. (Mainly Britains–Herald, Timpo and Elastolin, occasionally a few Greenwood & Ball, Lasset, Alymer or Segom: stock small and very variable)

Hummel's House of Miniatures, Burlington Arcade, Piccadilly, London, W1. (Courtenay–Ping, Greenwood & Ball, Ping, Sentry Box, Stadden)

Imperial Modellings, 7 St John Street, Lichfield, Staffs. (Historex, H–R, Lamming, Old Guard, Stadden, Valiant)

A. A. Johnston, Pitney, Langport, Somerset. (Military books, plates and cards)

Peter Kemplay, Framlingham, Woodbridge, Suffolk. (Cameron, Gammage, Hinchliffe, Historex, Lamming, Lasset, Phoenix, Series 77, Stadden, Surén)

The Northern Garrison, Castle Gate, Knaresborough. (Painting and diorama service)

James E. Luck Ltd, 34–6 High Street, Southgate, London, N14. (Old Britains, flats)

Model Figures and Hobbies, 8 College Square North, Belfast, N. Ireland. (Jackboot, Segom)

The Model Shop, 31 St Anne's Road, Harrow, Middlesex. (Almark, Garrison, Hinchliffe, Jacklex, Silvercross)

Price & Smith, 87 Mansfield Road, Nottingham. (Airfix, Almark, Helmet, Hinton, Historex, Jac, Jackboot, Lasset, Men o'War, Segom, Series 77, Stadden)

Regimental, 2 Castle Street, Kingston-upon-Thames, Surrey. (Almark, Gammage, Greenwood & Ball, Helmet, Hinchliffe, Hinton, Historex, Jackboot, Laing, Miniature Figurines, Phoenix, Stadden)

Seagull Model Ltd, 15 Exhibition Road, London, SW7. (Airfix, Almark, Aristo-Merité, Ciuffo (sole agent), Greenwood & Ball, Historex, Jac, Jackboot, Kirk, Laing, Men o'War, Phoenix, Segom, Series 77, Valiant, continental card model buildings)

Soldiers, 36 Kennington Road, London, SE1. (Airfix, Almark, Brunoe, Cameron, Cavalier, Douglas, Erikson, Gammage, Greenwood & Ball, Gottstein, Hinchliffe, Hinton, Historex, Imrie–Risley, Jac, Lamming, Men o'War, Mignot, Miniature Figurines, Neckel, Ochel, Old Guard, Phoenix, Romund, Scharlowsky, Segom, Series 77, Stadden, Surén, Tobinnus, Valiant, Warrior: Old Britains and other hollow-casts, solids and flats, wargame figures and games room)

Thingummies, 32–4 The Ridgeway, Wimbledon, London, SW19. (Small but esoteric collection of connoisseur models, constantly changing)

Tradition (Norman Newton incorporating Charles C. Stadden Ltd) 188 Piccadilly, London W1. (Arthur, Cameron, full range all series by Stadden, Tradition, wargame room, old solids and hollowcasts)

Under Two Flags, St. Christopher's Place, Wigmore Street, London W1. (Wide range of contemporary models, old Britains, Heyde, Mignot, and other historic models)

Shamus O. D. Wade, 37 Davis Road, Acton, London, W.3 (Mail-order – old Britains and their rivals and contemporaries, Heyde, Mignot etc)

ITALY

'Geco', via San G. B. de la Salle, 20132 Milan. (Italian and Spanish makers)

A. Soligo, via del Babuino 161, Rome. (Old models)

G. Testi, Corso Garibaldi, 2, Padua. (Old models)

SPAIN

'Chauve', Jorge Juan 31, Madrid I. (Spanish makers)

SWEDEN

John Maniatopoulos Hobby Service, Box 318 S–131 03 Nacka. (English and American contemporaries, Brunoe, Eriksson, Sivhed)

SWITZERLAND

P. Ruinart, rue des Terreaux 2, Lausanne, 1003. (Old models, paper sheets)

UNITED STATES

The Barefoot Soldier, 439 Meisel Avenue, Springfield, NJ, 07081. (Aristo-Merité, Bugle & Guidon, Cavalier, Lasset, Little Generals, Monarch, Phoenix, Rubin, Scale Specialities, Superior, Surén, TBS, Valiant, Vallance)

H. B. Charles & Son, 3213 Liberty Avenue, Pittsburgh, Pa, 15210. (Cameron, Cavalier, Gammage, GHQ, Hinchliffe, Jac, Jackboot, Lamming, Old Guard, Phoenix, Sanderson, Segom, Sentry Box, Series 77, Stadden, Superior)

Hobby Chest Inc, 615 Howard Street, Evanston, Illinois, 60202. (Aristo-Merité, Britains, Cameo, Elastolin, Gammage, Greenwood & Ball, Hinchliffe, Hinton, Historex, Imrie–Risley, Old Guard, Stadden, Superior)

Militaria, 103 The Quadrangle, 2800 Routh Street, Dallas, Texas, 75201. (Alcocer, Almirall, Aristo-Merité, Bugle & Guidon, Caldwell, Cameo, Cavalier, Covington, Gammage, Hinchliffe, Hinton, Historex, Imrie–Risley, Old Guard, Phoenix, Polland, Scott, Schrimshanders, Stadden, Stewart, Surén, Valiant, old commercial and connoisseur models)

Polk's Hobby Store, 314 Fifth Avenue, New York, NY, 10001. (Airfix, Alymer, Aristo-Merité, Cameo, Cavalier, Gammage, Historex, Imrie–Risley, Lasset, Old Guard, Rubin, Sanderson, Series 77, Soldat, Stadden)

The Soldier Shop, Inc, 1013 Madison Avenue, New York, NY, 10021. (Bugle & Guidon, Cameo, Cavalier, Hinchliffe, Historex, H–R, Imrie–Risley, Labayen, Old Guard, Segom, Series 77, Stadden, Stan Johansen, Superior, Valiant, Vallance, selected flats, cards, prints)

Waterloo Galleries, PO Box 4557, Irving, California, 92664. (Gordon, Stewart, Tubergen)

APPENDIX 3

Makers and manufacturers

Some makers, as well as placing their products with agents, are at the same time willing to sell direct to the public, whilst others, especially those who work to commission, or who employ a single agent, do not wish to have their addresses disclosed.

FRANCE

Historex Aeros SA, 23 rue Petion, Paris (and 3 Castle Street, Dover).

Mignot (CBG) 1 rue de Vieux Colombier, Paris.

GERMANY

Berliner Miniatur Plastiken (Walter Merten) 1 Berlin 42, Tempelhof, Industriestrasse, 25.

FLATS

Georg Cortum, 2000 Hamburg 71, Koppenstrasse 6.

Kurt Franke, 7410 Reutlingen, Aispachstrasse 23.

Rudolf Grünewald, 3001 Elze-Bennemühlen, Larchenweg 231b.

Wolfgang Hafer, 3511 Staufenberg-Landwehrhagen Raiffeisenstrasse 4.

Wolfgang Hodapp, 7500 Karlsruhe, Sophienstrasse 60.

Harald Kebbel, 8500 Nurnberg, Obere Schmiedgasse 56.

Hans Lecke, 3056 Rehburg, Brunnenstrasse 22.

Hans Müller, 6050 Offenbach/Main, Nordring 10.

Friedrich Neckel, 7321 Hattenhofen, Ledergasse 46.

Aloys Ochel, 2300 Kiel, Feldstrasse 24b.

Werner Otte, 3201 Barnten.

Heinz Pohl, A 1100 Wien X, Favoritenstrasse 133/3.

Alfred Retter, 7000 Stuttgart 75, Kleinhohenheimerstrasse 32.

Gunter Scharlowsky, 2800 Bremen 21, Auf den Hunnen 28.

Werner Scholtz, 1000 Berlin 12, Knesebeckerstrasse 86/87.

Gerhard Tobinnus, 3000 Hannover, Auf dem Dorn 24.

Johannes Trips, 7246 Empfingen 1, Reichenhalden 14.

H. Vorberg, 5300 Bonn, Rheinbacher Strasse 45.

Siegbert Wagner, 3000 Hannover-Linden, Limmerstrasse 65,

GREAT BRITAIN

Crown Miniatures Ltd (Ivor Pollock) Meadow Mill, Water Street, Portwood, Stockport, Cheshire.

Douglas Miniatures (J. D. Johnston) 16 Stafford Street, Leicester.

Frontier Models (A. Fermor) 7 Ludlow Close, Bletchley, Bucks and R. Leighton, 129 Windsor Road, Ilford, Essex.

Greenwood & Ball (W. F. Pearce) 61 Westbury St., Thornaby-on-Tees, Teesside. (Greenwood & Ball, Garrison, Lasset, Olive, Sanderson).

Helmet Products (D. Knight) Betchworth, Surrey.

Hinchliffe Models, Meltham, Huddersfield, Yorks (and Historex Agents, 3 Castle Street, Dover).

Hinton-Hunt Figures, 27 Camden Passage, Islington, London, N1.

Jac Models (J. A. & W. A. Collins) 56 High Street, East Grinstead, Sussex.

P. Laing, 11 Bounds Oak Way, Tunbridge Wells, Kent.

Miniature Figurines (N. Dickinson), 28/32 Northam Road, Southampton.

Minot (Barry) 20 Watling Street, Elstree, Herts.

Phoenix Model Developments Ltd (B. L. Marlow) The Square, Earls Barton, Northants.

Rose Miniatures (R. Gammage) 15 Llanover Road, London, SE18.

The Sentry Box (Yvonne Edmonds) 28 Carters Way, Wisborough Green, Billingshurst, Sussex.

Trophy Miniatures (M. John) 131 Plassey Street, Penarth, Glamorgan.

Warrior Metal Miniatures (H. Norey) 23 Grove Road, Leighton Buzzard.

Willie Figures (E. Surén) 60 Lower Sloane Street, London, SW1.

ITALY

F. Antonini, via Lago di Lesina 15, Rome.

A. Bormioli, 17041, Altare (SV).

ISA, viale del Carmine, Villa Viola 43, Luino (Varese).

SPAIN

J. Almirall, Rosellon 285 bis, Barcelona.

Alymer (Angel Comez Placentia) Gral. Queipo de Llano, 119, Burjasot, Valencia.

R. Labayen, Avenida de Navarra L, San Sebastian.

L. Saez-Alcocer, Calle Ciegas de San Cucufate no 1, Bajos, Barcelona, 3.

SWEDEN

H. Eriksson, Sommarrovagen 8, Karlstad.

UNITED STATES

Aristo-Merité Miniatures, 314 Fifth Avenue, New York, NY, 10001.

Bugle & Guidon (Thomas E. Bookwalter and Stanley E. Glanzer) PO Box 248, West Carrollton, Ohio 45449.

Cameo Miniatures (Coulter–Bennett, Ltd) North Hollywood, California.

Cavalier Miniatures Ltd (Allan Silk and Edward Lober) 105 Jamaica Avenue, Brooklyn, NY, 11207.

H–R Products (Cy Broman), 9232 Waukegan Road, Morton Grove, Illinois, 60053.

Imrie–Risley Miniatures Inc, 425a Oak Street, Copiague, NY, 11726.

K & L Company (Thomas Figures), PO Box 1844, Baton Rouge, La. 70821.

Monarch Miniatures (A. J. Benkert) 41–33 50th Street, Woodside, NY, 11377.

Old Guard Inc (W. H. Murray) PO Box 2806, Plainfield, NJ, 07062 (and at Rothbury, Northumberland).

Jack Scruby, 2044 S. Linwood, Visalia, California, 93277.

Soldiers Unlimited (Michael Ferguson) 813 Elliston Drive, Wyndmoor, Pa, 19118.

Squadron/Rubin, 3515 E. 10 Mile Road, Warren, Michigan, 48091.
Stan Johansen Miniatures, 41–4 Ridge Road, Naugatuck, Conn, 06770.
Valiant Miniatures (Arthur Neckermann) PO Box 394, Skokie, Illinois, 60076.
Vallance Miniatures (Rogean Advertising Associates) PO Box 1776, Springfield, NJ, 07081.

APPENDIX 4
Notes on Prices

Most collectors have to budget for their purchases, and the following notes may be of assistance in assessing what they will have to pay for models.

Alkathene models are available in most shops at a few pence or cents, but some of the better plastic models cost more. Starlux, for example, will cost 75p ($2) foot, and £1.25 ($3.15) mounted, Elastolin 85p ($2.05) and £1.75 ($4.50), Airfix 25p (62c), Historex 80p ($2.50) and £1.65 ($4.25), Helmet 60p ($1.52).

Wargame models are most reasonable in price, and vary very little from maker to maker. Basically, any model up to 25mm costs about 8p (20c) foot, and 20p (50c) mounted, with artillery up to about £1 ($2.55). Models in 30–45mm size average 50p ($1.35) to £1.25 ($3.25) according to quality.

Flats, obtainable from continental dealers, average 25p (65c) to 50p ($1.35), artillery and composite pieces costing up to £2 ($5.05) each. If one is unfortunate, customs duties and VAT have to be added to these if imported into England.

Makers of 54mm models realise that they have to be competitive, and by and large unpainted castings, sometimes in kit form, remain fairly uniform in most parts of the world. An uncomplicated foot soldier will cost between 90p ($2.45) to £2 ($5.05) but certain ranges, such as standard bearers, motorcyclists, and the like, where extra equipment is required, may be priced up to £3.50 ($9). Mounted troops are proportionately more expensive, usually ranging from £4 to £5 ($10.85 to $13) to £10 ($27.25) or even to £15 ($39.75). Customs duties and VAT have also to be added if ordered direct from abroad. Artillery and groups of mounted models cost up to £50 ($130).

A number of makers supply their models already painted, and here the prices range from £2.35 ($6) to £4.50 ($12). When, however, a maker employs a painter to do this, the result costs four to five times the price of an unpainted casting.

As examples of the larger models, Series 77 charge £2.15

($5.50) for a casting, and £6.45 ($17) for a mounted figure. Their chariot is £19.50 ($50); Stadden 90mm models are £2.80 ($7) painted £7.50 ($20); Cameron 120mm £6.25 ($16) and £9.25 ($25) respectively; Superior Models, castings, $14 (£5.45), Little Generals, castings, $12.50 (£5).

A number of makers, such as Berdou, des Fontaines, and the like, work only to commission, and arrangements have to be made with them direct. It is safe to say that one could not obtain a model from them for under £50 for a foot soldier. Indeed, I recently saw an advertisement in a journal stating the willingness of a certain somewhat obscure freelance artist to undertake commissions on the basis of £50 for a foot figure and £75 for a mounted one.

With models of historic interest it is difficult to give any real guide lines. A Courtenay footsoldier may well fetch £8 ($21) and a mounted one from £25 ($65) to £35 ($90) at auction, but one can purchase a Courtenay–Ping at Hummels for £6 ($16) to £12 ($32). (Ping himself is most modest in his charges.) One would expect to pay about £2 ($5.50) for a Carman, £3 ($8) for an original Greenwood & Ball, Mignots are available in France from the makers at between £3 ($8) and £10 ($27), whilst if a Lucotte came on the market the price might well double this. Heyde and the like occur regularly in lists and shops at from £3 ($8) to £10 ($27), with bands etc, fetching between £50 ($130) and £75 ($190). Vertunnis are priced at the equivalent of £9 ($25) in Paris. Britains form a category on their own, and prices vary considerably according to condition, rarity and snobbery. One sees them at prices ranging from £1 ($2.55) to £5 ($12.95), the rarer ones from £15 ($40) to £20 ($52), wheeled transport being considerably higher. Hollow-casts other than Britains are priced considerably less, averaging 50p ($1.35) to £5 ($12.95) for the more uncommon models.

Old flats again, are extremely variable, depending upon where they are for sale. The prolific makers such as Heinrichsen are quite frequently found, and they should not cost more than about 30p (75c) each, but some antique shops charge disproportionate prices. The flats of such makers as Gottstein and du Bois at auction would fetch about £4 ($10.85) each, whilst collective groups, such as Swiss villages, parks and garden scenes, and the like, sell at about £50 ($130) the set.

Pre-war Elastolin figures have a following in some circles, and models in good condition fetch from about £2 to £3 each. The most desirable are those in large sets complete with, say, pontoons or waggons, or the collection of Adolf Hitler and his henchmen.

It should be noted that prices of new models will vary according to the financial conditions prevailing at any given time.

A number of makers with a limited output may take a considerable time to fulfil their orders from agents, who do not always stock the full range. More time still will be taken for ordering models from other countries.

ACKNOWLEDGEMENTS

I wish to thank a large number of model soldier makers who have, by their unstinting help, made this book possible. Many were so kind as to send me actual specimens, at times in considerable quantities. My regret is that I am not able to illustrate them in the number that I would have wished.

The information they gave me was supplemented by the following agents and dealers, all of whom spent much of their time in answering my many queries, or by sending me lists, catalogues or actual models: Peter Blum, The Soldier Shop; William Connolly, Waterloo Galleries; Robert Cowan, Militaria; J. Fualdes, Historex; Peter Greenhill, Thingummies; A. Griffiths, Tradition; Peter Kemplay, The Northern Garrison; W. Kirkness, Models & Militaria; C. K. McCarthy, Soldiers; John Maniatopoulos, Hobby Service; B. L. Marlow, Phoenix Model Developments; A. W. Neckermann, Valiant Miniatures; W. F. Pearce, Greenwood & Ball; L. Pierce, K. & L. Company; Dennis Teague, The Armoury; John Tunstill, Soldiers; David Winter, The Old Guard.

Other valuable help was received from the following: M. Alberini; J. Almirall; R. Anderson; R. Gennari; M. Hundleby; and Don and Honey Ray.

The greatest enthusiasm and support came from Bob Cowan, Bill Connolly, W. F. Greer, Major Robert Rowe and Valentine Bean, whilst Victor C. Norman (The Barefoot Soldier) went beyond the line of duty in order to give me a detailed insight into the models currently made in the United

States, and Allan Silk (Cavalier) and Arthur Neckermann (Valiant) both sent me most generous quantities of their productions. I also have to thank A. A. Johnston for his help over books of uniform references, and to George Allen & Unwin Ltd for permission to quote from the late J. R. R. Tolkien's *The Lord of the Rings*.

INDEX

Page numbers in italic refer to illustrations